No Accountability

Keith Lawton

First published in the United Kingdom

by Copyhouse Press Ltd

Copyhouse Press Ltd

International House, 24 Holborn Viaduct, London,

United Kingdom, EC1A 2BN

ISBN **9781911340041**

A Memoir and a True Story

Table of Contents

Preface

Born to, what was described as, an alcoholic father and a schizophrenic mother, I was taken into care from my mother's arms at birth, myself and my brothers being frequently left home alone. After that, I alternated between living in council care and at my parents' house until the age of five when my father died. I was then placed in care full-time.

No Accountability is the follow up to my debut book *No Photographs*. It tells a true story, written only by myself, not an outside author trying to put their own slant on my life. Parts are heavily based on my memories as a child, such as the time I spent with my biological family and in care, as I had few other references to go by. I have tried to present the true-life facts of my story as best I can.

I am totally aware that there are a lot of very good caring and professional people working in care today, and that the incidents I was involved in are from a different era – taking place almost 50 years ago. That said, this delicate subject needs to be broached, not only to raise awareness of what happened in the past, but to encourage those who were involved to admit their wrongs. I hope this book will help highlight some of Society's past failings and allow certain people to move on.

This is to help people change, stop stereotyping others and to realise that speaking up is the correct and moral thing to do. This doesn't just mean it's exclusively sexual abuse to children or others. It's more than that. It's mental and/or physical abuse and control involving all ages, creeds, races, abilities, whether it happens within a matrimonial setting, close family circles, or in care. I share, of course, my slant on my own experiences of abuse from being bought up in council care (having to endure the degradation of glorified child slavery), as well as later being the physiological and psychological victim in marriage. It's the failure to speak out, more often than not, which causes more problems for the victim as this invariably leads to a tendency to shoot the messenger. I hope people appreciate what a difficult and brave thing it is to do to go public, but, by not confronting this abuse, the controller is given more power to control.

Perpetrators of abuse in all forms need to come forward, publicly admit to their failings and be held accountable for their actions. Although some lose their jobs and go to prison, most never confess to what they did or apologise face to face with their prey. It is morally unacceptable for them not to speak out. And normal people, the 'average Joes', also need to lose the stigma they have around people who have suffered abuse in the past. Everyone has just as much right to live on this planet. People have to accept their failings and the failings of other people, and commit to learning from them. Doing so will help change humanity for the better.

I haven't got the strength, time or inclination to gain justice from those who abused me, and, besides, I don't think it would do anyone any good. *No Accountability* was not written to gain justice for myself, but is instead aimed at giving strength to others who have been through similar experiences, encouraging them to release their demons. Read it, share it, review it, comment on it and put air under the wings of truth and send it aloft. If everyone tells their story, then together we will win.

Horace and Angela Mary

Horace Lawton and Angela Mary Rogers met in Wolverhampton at a dance in 1958. Horace had six brothers and one sister, and they all lived together at their mother's house, 48 Oaklands Green, Bilston, West Midlands. The house was in a poor council estate that was set in a crescent. The Lawtons were lucky enough to have their very own massive lattice-structured electricity pylon practically right outside their house – the cables clicking away, giving out radiation. Lovely and picturesque. The neighbours must have been so jealous. It was what probably frazzled my dad's brain cells at an early age.

Horace's mother and father – Alice and William – had a son called Lesley (Lez), who sadly died at a young age, and was buried quite local at Bilston Cemetery on the 9th of June, 1952 at twenty-three years old. He was the first to be buried in, what was to become, a family grave. No parent expects or contemplates burying their child before their time, let alone two of their children.

Angela Mary Rogers was born on the 4th of August, 1936, and her parents were Joseph H. Rogers and Hilda Rogers – formerly Robinson. They had three daughters and three sons. Angela Mary Rogers lived about ten miles away from Horace in Codsall. She lived at her parents' house, Birches Bungalow, in Birches Bridge,

Codsall – which is in the district of Bilston. The bungalow was on a main road opposite a busy railway line and close to the railway station. To the back of the bungalow was a large long garden that was full of fruit trees. Angela's mother and father were keen gardeners and wrapped apples in paper to store for the winter in cool parts of the house. They also made preserves with softer fruits, and blanched and froze the green vegetables from the garden.

Horace had been courting Angela for a few years, and they were not having the best of luck financially, when Angela fell pregnant with their first son Brian. Oops. It was time to get things sorted in the marriage department.

Horace was a 33-year-old bachelor and constructional painter, and he married Angela Mary Rogers, a 22-year-old spinster, on 27th June, 1959 at the Bilston register office. Horace was the son of William Lawton, a deceased tin smith, whilst Angela Mary Lawton was the daughter of Joseph Henry Rogers, a tyre builder. He and Angela's sisters were witnesses to the marriage. It was a quiet affair, although both Horace and Angela had extended families in the local area.

Newlyweds Horace and Angela went off to Blackpool for their honeymoon for a long weekend while she was heavily pregnant. They went to the Tower Ballroom, where they drank tea, danced and had a wonderful time. Fish and chips seemed to taste better by the sea, and the big bands playing in the Tower Ballroom knocked them for six with awe. The Pleasure Beach arcades, slot machines and rides mesmerised them, the weather was good and most importantly they were together.

Their first-born son, Brian Lawton, was born on the 30th of July 1959, at New Cross Hospital in Wolverhampton. Brian's birth certificate was registered at the house of my gran and granddad, on my father's side, at 48 Oaklands Green.

Angela and Horace's second son, Stephen Lawton, was born on the 4th of July, 1960 at 22 Bignor Street, Cheetham, Lancashire. He was again recorded as the son of Horace Lawton, a painter, and his wife Angela Mary Lawton, formerly Rogers.

Angela and Horace went to find work in Manchester as Bill, the husband of Angela's sister Velma, had gotten work in Rochdale. Angela and Velma as sisters were very close, and you need solid friends when you're not the richest person in monetary terms and have a growing young family. Angela also suffered from a mental illness, which was later to be diagnosed as schizophrenia. Her brother Chris later told me that they didn't know this at the time, and that there was no proper name for Angela's illness. Angela didn't cope well with life in general, but having a big extended family helped compensate a bit, and acted as a safety net for her when she fell. Horace worked long hours on construction sites that were sometimes an hour-plus travel away. When you have a young family, you have to step up to the plate and bring in that much needed cash.

Velma and Bill later moved to Scotland to work in the North Sea oil industry, and so Angela and Horace moved back to the West Midlands. As Horace and Angela had a young family, no real work and no money, moving to the West Midlands, where they had extended family, was the only sensible option open to them. Horace and Angela managed to get a council house at Pace Crescent in Bilston, an area they both knew well, and that was near both of their extended families. Horace found work as an industrial painter, painting existing and newly built factories and offices. The pay for an industrial painter wasn't ground breaking or stratospheric, but it was adequate to provide for his wife and young family – just about.

Angela and Horace had their third son (me) on the 4th of February, 1965, and I was born at New Cross Hospital in Wolverhampton. The house at Pace Crescent was another three-bedroom semi-detached one, and pretty much a carbon copy of Horace's parents' house at 48 Oaklands Green. It was the last place where we all lived as a family before Dad's accident on the 6th of June, 1970. This catastrophic accident tore our family apart, and I am still trying to find the missing pieces to this day.

My brothers, Brian and Stephen, burned my potty on the open coal fire when I was little. I remember screaming as I tried to rescue my red plastic poo station.

The commotion that followed was crazy, and somehow between us we managed to set fire to the armchair. I remember the ablaze chair being manhandled out into the back garden. You certainly need 24-hour, 360° vision surveillance when you're watching three boys under the age of ten. My Farley's rusk biscuits would be prised from me and eaten by my brothers, and I was frequently put into makeshift go-karts and pushed from the top of the hill on our road. Each time they made sure that they provided enough momentum to propel me at a speed that would undoubtedly cause the go-kart to overturn and be wrecked. I'd get straw shoved up my sleeves and be made to go around begging, 'penny for the guy' and 'come on, mister,' even having to sing carols at Christmas. Anything to get a few pence so my brothers could buy sweets and cigarettes. Player's No.6 was their preferred brand, with Woodbine being a second preference.

As children we'd be out for hours, just as all the kids on the estate and across the country would be. We'd be in the woods constructing dens, treehouses, swings and bike ramps. We'd wait for the ice cream van in the summer as it sent out its music-box tune over the loudspeaker. The sound of it would ensure you were already salivating when the van was two streets away. We would beg for money to get a 99 with a flake, raspberry juice, chopped nuts, and 100s & 1000s sprinkled on top. If we weren't waiting for that, then it would be for the milkman to come around. We would try to swipe bottles of Corona Pop from the back of the slow-moving electric float – with dandelion and burdock being the preferred flavour. Managing to nick a bottle of milk as well was a bonus. On Wednesday evenings the fish and chips van would come around. The fact that the fish and chips were wrapped in old newspaper somehow seemed to give them a better taste.

We would go to town on Saturday mornings to attend the matinee at the Odeon cinema in Wolverhampton. It would be either *Champion the Wonder Horse*, *Flash Gordon* or *The Lone Ranger Rides Again* – always in black and white. Whichever it was, the film would keep us glued to our seats, and we'd have popcorn and ice cream to munch on if we'd been able to get enough deposit money from the pop bottles that we'd nicked or found. I think you got around three old pence for each intact empty bottles that you returned – so you would soon have enough money for sweets and cigarettes if you trawled for empties effectively enough. The television set we had was rented from Granada and had a slot where you put your money in – it was two shillings, about 10p in new money. These televisions were later changed to allow 50 pence pieces after decimalisation on 15th February, 1971, but an event out of our control meant that we were never able to be together as a family after Friday the 3rd of July, 1970, when my father's funeral took place.

The football pools man would call around to collect the tear-off slip from the coupon, the insurance man would come around, the 'never-never' man would come to collect money for the furniture we had on hire, a man would come to collect money for the twin tub washing machine and peddlers would come door to door selling all manner of stuff. There was also the mobile shop, the mobile fruit and vegetable shop, the mobile fish man, the mobile meat man, the milkman, the rag-and-bone man and the dreaded library bus – all coming around regularly. With all these people, and the neighbours and the neighbours' kids coming in and out of our house freely, it was always busy. I think our house would've been busy enough with just our family. I was only five years old at that time, but I remember some things from that period. They were good times.

My mother, Angela, woke up as per usual on Friday the 5th of June, 1970. She got up and went down stairs to get breakfast ready for my father, and then made him a packed lunch with a thermos flask of tea for his brew-time at work. Dad got up and had his porridge and bacon sandwich, and Mum had a quick chat with him before she began to prepare breakfast for the kids. It was payday, the weekend was knocking on the door and the summer weather was fine. The washing was out and the kids were still in bed, and so my mother and father stole a few last precious moments together.

Mum said goodbye to Dad and saw him to the front door as he went to get on with his work. She collected three bottles of milk from outside the door and headed back in to make porridge for her lads, her babies, her world. She emptied the cold teapot's contents onto the rhubarb plant just outside the back door and sat down to have a cigarette, contemplating the day and planning what she would do with her family over the weekend. Mum hung out the washing that was in the twin-tub washer and refuelled it with another load. It was June and already 20°C, so there was no need to squeeze them and run them through the mangle. Another cigarette and a couple more cups of tea later, she emptied the contents of a second teapot onto the mountain of tealeaves amassing on the poor rhubarb plant.

Angela shouted up the stairs, 'Come on, you lazy lot – get up,' put the kettle on and got the table ready for her boys. It was just Stephen and Brian. I was too young for school, and so I got to lie in and have Mum all to myself when I was eventually prised from my slumber. Stephen and Brian got up, brushed their teeth together and went downstairs to eat. With their breakfasts finished, Stephen and Brian were sent to school – but first they were subjected to a warm soapy flannel being rubbed around their necks and ears.

'Right, off you go, be good and don't mess around on your way home. Fish and chips tonight.'

The table was cleared, and I was woken up and made to get ready for my day with Mum. Most of the time we'd go to the park to feed the ducks, which was only a short walk away. The ducks would merrily swim around the half-submerged shopping trollies and peck at the rubbish that the wind had blown into the water. That day would turn out to be very different from the norm – it would be a day to remember. Angela got my breakfast ready, sorted my clothes out for the day, got the washing off the line and put another load from the twin-tub washer out to dry. With all of the washing done, the twin-tub would not get fed again until Dad got home from work, and my two brothers, the dreaded twosome, got back from school later that day. After getting out of bed, I of course received the flannel treatment on my neck and ears just like my brothers.

Mum cleared the table and started to do the washing up as I ate. Another pot of tea was nearly finished, and soon more tealeaves would be added to the mound on the rhubarb plant. While I went upstairs to get out of my pyjamas and get dressed for our day out, Mum sat in peace and enjoyed another cigarette. When I was ready, we went off to the local shop to get some stuff with the money that was left over from Dad's wages from the week before, such as bread and shillings for the TV, the gas and the electric. Everyone was after shillings on the poor council estates. Often people couldn't get enough of them as shopkeepers rarely had many. There were also frequent power cuts, and so we had to buy candles, matches, firelighters and coal.

We headed home with the pram that was used as a shopping trolley, and got ready to go to my cousin's house. Angela spent about an hour chatting. It was an excuse for more tea drinking and another couple of cigarettes. Mum and Dad were big smokers – I think most people were in those days. Both of my parents had a lot of close family in the area, and everyone on those estates lived in each other's pockets. We popped in and out of people's homes, and people did the same with our house. It was good to go somewhere where you could get a jam sandwich or a handful of currents.

We were just about to make our way back home, Mum was finishing yet another cup of tea, when one of my cousins came charging in like a rhinoceros on steroids shouting, 'The police are outside your house.'

When Mum and I got back to Pace Crescent, we saw that the police were indeed outside our house. Mum just suspected that Stephen and Brian had been up to no good, or that one of them had had an accident. She hurried her pace and asked the police what they were doing outside her home. On hearing the news, Mum crumpled and fell to the floor, crying and wailing uncontrollably; my mother had suffered with mental health problems for years, and this blow was too much. The police told my mum that her husband Horace had had an accident at work and had been taken to the hospital as a result. They didn't know the full details, but Dad was in a bad way and they suspected that he didn't have much longer left to live. Mum was told to fear the worst, and we both got into the police car and were driven to Shropshire Orthopaedic Hospital, which was about 25 miles away. It took us about 35 minutes to get there, which felt like a lifetime.

The police dropped Mum and me off outside Shropshire Orthopaedic Hospital, and we went in to try to find Horace. We were told we couldn't see him at first, and that the nurse would come and get us when he was ready. The nurse came out and took us to a small side-room where I saw my dad – he was strapped down on a wheeled hospital bed and looked like he was in great pain. The nurse explained that Dad had broken his back in a fall at work. Dad was an industrial painter and it turned out he had fallen off a ladder. I remember so well that Dad was screaming and Mum was holding him and talking to him as best she could. Dad had straps across his feet, his waist, his chest, his arms and even one across his forehead. They were to keep his back restrained and to keep him in position.

Dad looked at me with pain in his eyes, screaming. In order to see his face, I had to stand on my tiptoes. For years after, I had nightmares of that moment. It was only when I received his death certificate 42 years later that I found out where they came from. That is when the nightmares stopped. Night after night, I saw his face, the face of a man whom I did not know, reaching out to me and looking straight into my eyes while screaming. Not the best memory to have of your dad, and I am so grateful now, in later life, that the nightmares have finally stopped.

Dad died of a heart attack in the early hours of the following day, Saturday the 6th of June, 1970. He was only 44 years of age – no age for a man to die, no age for a dad to die and no age for a husband to be lost by her wife.

My mother was 33 years old at the time, so looking back she was only a kid herself. Angela Mary's life fell apart and she went into a tailspin. She wasn't able to deal with things well at all. My uncle Chris later said to me that at the time they didn't know what Mum was suffering from, but they knew she wasn't at all well mentally. The term schizophrenia was coined in 1910 by Swiss doctor Paul Eugen Bleuler, but I'm not quite sure how widely used and recognised it was in the UK in 1970. It was the electric shock treatment for people suffering from mental health issues in those days. They would also lock them up in a lunatic asylum for being only mildly ill. The Earth was still flat in the eyes of most people, I think.

On the day of my dad's funeral, Wednesday the 24th of June, 1970, we left my granny's house and walked the short distance to the hearse and funeral cars that were parked up on the straighter bit of road just off the crescent. The streets of the council estate were lined with people, and I remember hearing them say, 'How awful, those poor kids,' but I was too young to realise why they were even there at all, let alone comprehend what they were saying. We got into the car behind the hearse and were driven a short distance in the funeral procession to Bilston Cemetery. My father's coffin was carried to the grave and lowered down. Words were said over him, and the coffin was overlaid with flowers and then covered with earth. I don't remember much about the burial, but with such a large extended family on both sides there must have been quite a crowd there.

Blackpool

After my dad's funeral, my mother tried to act strong and carry on – like you're supposed to. However, with three young children under 11 years old, and her mental health problems being worsened by her recent loss, it soon became apparent to those close to her that she needed a few days away from familiar surroundings. Mum's family clubbed together enough money for her to have a few days away, so that she could grieve with her boys and come to terms with the loss of her husband. Mum was in a really bad way and understandably so. She thought she'd fallen as far as she could possibly fall and suffered as much as she possibly could – but there was still more to come.

Mum thought about the proposal to get away for a few days and finally decided we should go to Blackpool. I suppose she thought she could rekindle old memories of her newly departed husband, as it was where they had spent their honeymoon together just over ten years earlier. We had moved into her dad's bungalow in Codsal temporarily – in a bid for Mum to regain her strength and composure – and had to return home to 27 Pace Crescent briefly to get some clothes and the two suitcases she had left there. Once we'd gotten what we needed, we went back to Granddad's. He took me and my brothers out of harm's way into his big long back garden while Mum prepared herself for the trip, washing and ironing enough clothes for herself and us lads.

After the two suitcases were filled, she came out to the garden to collect us from the close eye of Granddad. She met us with a bowl of warm soapy water and the dreaded flannel. Ears, knees, arms, the backs of our necks were all given the flannel treatment – it was like getting a bed bath whilst standing upright. Mum and Granny walked the short distance to the railway station – it was quite literally across the road – looked at the timetable and booked the cheapest tickets. They then returned to Grandad's house so that Mum could collect her boys.

We said our goodbyes as if we were leaving forever – and it turned out that wasn't too far from the truth. We walked the short distance to the train station and excitedly set off for Blackpool on the morning of Thursday the 2nd of July, 1970. The journey was to take just over two hours, with there being a short stop in Manchester. We were all so excited, gawking out of the windows of the carriage. Mum took us on a quick trip to the buffet bar to order some cups of Lipton's tea, because nothing's quite right unless you have copious amounts of tea. The world just wouldn't turn without it. Mum sat quietly, contemplating and puffing on her cigarette. What things were churning around in her mind, I will never know – cherished memories, worries about what the future might hold, how she would cope... I suppose everything and anything but going to Blackpool was on her mind.

Upon arriving at Blackpool, Mum trawled for a place for us to stay until Monday morning – when we were due to return to the West Midlands. Finally, after lugging the two heavy bulging suitcases around for ages, Mum booked us all into a boarding house. It was much to our relief as we were all bushed from the trip. We just wanted anywhere to stay – to enable us to explore our new surroundings for the rest of the afternoon. After we'd finished unpacking and hanging up our clothes, and had set up the 'Z beds', we went out to visit the Pleasure Beach arcades. We played on the penny falls and went on the waltzers, the bumper cars and a few other rides. By the end of the evening, we were all worn out, and so we headed back to the bed & breakfast to hit the hay.

We got up the following day and did the tooth-brushing routine, all taking it in turns to use the small sink in the bedroom. Next, it was – guess what? – more of the flannel routine. When we were all made presentable, and our hair was combed, spat on and combed some more, we left our little room and went down for our breakfast. We asked for as much tea and toast and marmalade as the landlady would allow. Once we'd finished eating, off we went to the pier for a spot of crab fishing, and the beach for a spot of paddling and sandcastle making. Mum bought a small inflatable dingy, which she and my brothers took turns to blow up. Once it was inflated, Brian and Stephen sent me off on my first ever voyage. This nearly ended in disaster. I was blown out away from the shore while my brothers stood there laughing – then they realised how far I was going out. A man in a boat came to rescue me and the cheap blow-up dingy. After that we had our obligatory donkey rides, with Mum being sure to keep us away from the sea. We weren't to be trusted – lads are lads. Your appetite runs riot at the seaside, and after another day of sea air, we all decided to have some fish and chips.

We found a fish and chip shop and ordered four lots to go, as well as a bottle of dandelion and burdock pop. We walked a little, as it was a lovely July evening, but it was so busy along the seafront that it was almost impossible to locate a bench that would seat all four of us. Eventually we managed to find a quiet area, away from all the other families. Once we sat down, we opened up our newspaper-wrapped bounty, got out the ketchup and got stuck into our fish and chips with our fingers. Fish and chips seem to taste so much better when eaten in sea air. After we'd finish eating and swilled our food down with dandelion and burdock, we were cleaned up by Mum and her flannel. Where she got a damp flannel from I'll never know; she must have had a secret pocket with a flannel in a plastic bag – the woman should have been a magician. It would have been far better if she'd pulled out a teapot and four cups. Tea is everything – it quenches thirst and comforts you like nothing else. We packed our stuff, scrunched up the waste newspaper, and Brian and Stephen were tasked with going to put it in the bin.

While Brian and Stephen were gone, only about a hundred yards away, some men walked towards me and Mum while we were still sitting on the bench. A couple of the men seemed to know my mum, they were from the West Midlands, and they started chatting to us. The men were asking how her husband Horace was and things started to get out of hand – they started pushing my mum to the ground. I didn't know what was happening and I was screaming louder than my mother was. Brian and Stephen came running back in an attempt to protect my mum, but ended up getting hit, punched and pushed away. The so-called men eventually ran off when they had each in turn had their way with my poor broken-hearted mother – leaving her on the pavement like a piece of discarded rubbish, like the used fish and chips paper that my brothers had thrown in the bin. They left us three kids sobbing over our mum's collapsed body. She did what she knew how to do best: she got up, she got strong and she tried to take her babies back home. She left all of our things in the guest house, and, distraught, made her way to the railway station with us in tow.

Personally, I am not after retribution as this time has long since passed me by. That said, there is great comfort in knowing that those men will suffer for eternity down below in burning fire, being constantly prodded and poked by the horned red man with his trident. I know they will never confess their wrongs to themselves, let alone stand up in a court of law and publically testify before their god. Cowards like them are much of a muchness; they just don't have the balls to do the decent thing.

My mum and us three brothers got the train from Blackpool back to the West Midlands, then, somehow, we ended up going from the West Midlands back to Blackpool. Mum had suffered a breakdown and went into freefall. Her schizophrenia didn't help, and, like anyone would in that situation, she fell apart like a dried leaf on a windy Autumn day. Eventually she was brought to the attention of a British transport policeman.

He noticed that there was something not quite right with how we were all acting as a family and got us off at the next railway station. The transport police called through to the local police, and my mum was carted off – literally by the men in white coats. She was subsequently put into a mental asylum. Mum must have endured a lifetime of mental and physical trauma, and the pain of losing her beloved Horace and her three young boys, her babies, must have been unimaginable. I never saw my mother again, and so at the age of five years old, I had already lost both of my parents.

They didn't think my mother was fit to take care of us, but they were so very wrong. We should have been left financially secure from my father's accident, and the state should have made sure our mum stayed with us and had all of the help that she needed to look after her babies. My two brothers and I were put into council care homes – and this is just how nice they are – and we were split up to protect our feelings. I will never understand how they thought that made sense. You can only get proper care and love from your own family – anything else is just synthetic.

The upset of that decision has followed me through my life, through 50 years, and will most likely haunt me until the day I die. I do hope these writings will make it ease a little, and I hope that this testimony helps others. Nevertheless, most of all I hope this book pierces the incredibly hard shells of the magistrates, the state, the public sector – and their care staff – and the general public. They need to turn their denial of their failures into positive teachings, so that they can educate others and ensure that what happened to me never happens again to anyone else. I can tell you there is good in those people, as there is in all mortals, but attitudes do still need to change.

Procedures that were in place were no doubt followed to the letter, but if a procedure doesn't apply to what is actually happening then it is no good. If people don't admit their failings, then they cannot learn to help others. Investigating failure is the best opportunity for learning available. We learn from our mistakes, but only if we accept that we messed up. People's behavioural traits need to change, and they need to get more involved in their work. They need to deviate, ask questions, question themselves, seek advice and commit to continual improvement. They need to remember that they are dealing with people and not things.

Many of the children that go into council care have been through a life of pain and hurt. They have been neglected by their parents for multiple reason – their parents were either drug or alcohol dependant, abusers, too old, too young, too poor, too sick or just couldn't be bothered to look after them. Some people can just walk away and leave their children without a backwards glance, simply because they are mentally ill, physically challenged, not of the right sex or purely just unwanted. They have already suffered enough. The government have a duty to look after the children that come into council care, and it is unforgiveable that so many children, like myself, have been failed.

Taken into Council Care

My brothers and I were taken to a council care home in Wednesfield called Braybrook, which has long since closed. It was a big Victorian workhouse/prison-like building, and wasn't fit for its purpose; the very name Braybrook made it sound hard and prison-like. The home has since been linked to a catalogue of complaints, with there being accusations of mistreatment and abuse of the children that were incarcerated within those walls. From Braybrook we all got separated into different care homes. We were apparently split up for our own good, as it would apparently be less mentally damaging for us if we were simply to forget each other.

Later on, I would dig, probe, poke and research until I found the truth of what happened to us. We had just lost our father due to an accident at work, and we had just lost our loving mother as the state had ruled her to be unfit to look after us three young boys. Separating us did none of us any good whatsoever – even 50 years on it still defies my sense of logic and tears my heart apart, occasionally causing me to fold up and cry. The love you get from your paternal family is far greater than any synthetic love – we needed each other.

My mother had three sisters and three brothers, and my father had two sisters and six brothers, meaning that my uncles and aunties amounted to thirteen. But none of them stepped forward to care for us lads – even though some of them didn't even have children of their own. It still tortures me today, totally defying all of my moral comprehension. If they didn't want us, they could have at least cared for their own sister. I'm not bitter here, I just do not understand, that's all. There is no way I can make excuses for those people, because however hard I try to justify their actions – no matter what avenue I take, and whatever off-the-wall theory I concoct – I cannot come to a conclusion that explains why they wouldn't look after their own family. All of that is bad enough, but for them to not even contact us or let us know we were in their thoughts was even worse. We didn't receive any letters, Christmas cards or birthday cards from our own relatives. It stinks.

The chinless, faceless state with its chinless, faceless, form-ticking experts decided to separate us lads into different care homes, and so Brian went off to a home in Oswestry and my brother Stephen went off to a home in Bath. I was resigned to staying in the West Midlands. They should have just put down their generic forms and looked each of us in the eye. I wonder what decisions they would have made then?

It wrenches at my heart every day to think about what those unfeeling, posh, aloof, uppity, do-gooder, faceless, form-ticking people did to us without any reprisal – without even a backward glance. Would they do that to their own children, I wonder? They forgot us, put us down as statistics and threw away the key.

At five years old, I would never see my mother, father or my brother Brian ever again. I was scared, confused and messed up in the head – I just couldn't understand what had happened. The deep pain I felt cannot be taught by a book – it cannot be learned in any way shape or form. It is something that cannot be remotely understood by the detached people that controlled my life. Those aloof hypocrites who were so far detached from reality as to leave a confused, frightened five-year-old child to the mercy of their so-called care homes, their perverse staff, their wild children and the satanic governess Mrs Davenport without feeling and without a backward glance. I hope those people are having sleepless nights, because I still do nearly 50 years later. I do not say this in spite, but in the hope that they learn how to change their practice for the better, and for the benefit of other disadvantaged people who cross their paths.

These people, through their education, had suspicion bred into them and caring bred out of them. For them, all those children were just part of some big social experiment. They got no reprisal for their actions, and they are so aloof that, even if you showed them the facts, they wouldn't recognise their own failings. They would twist their mistakes, and try to justify them and spin them off as markers of how good and precise their judgement was with the evidence they had at that time. They would not retract their horns or admit to their failures under any circumstances. This is the same attitude that abusers take – and isn't that what they really were?

Any child that is subject to multiple changes – going to multiple schools, having a catalogue of foster parents, being pushed from pillar to post – all after losing their paternal family is surely going to be greatly damaged. Although there are many different reasons why young people end up in care homes, none should be treated as if they are criminals. When they are at their most vulnerable, they shouldn't be exposed to wild children that have turned feral, who see violence as the norm, or perverse members of staff. There's a demonstration of how unfeeling they were, I'm still calling them 'members of staff'. Their treatment of children only leads to rebellion and cries for help during their incarceration, and even more so when they are turned out onto the street when they turn 18. I hope they do raise the age of release to 21, but it will not really make any difference if the pre-care isn't there… It isn't rocket science.

I was terrified, confused and probably waling like a banshee when I received that first of many injustices, but I can say now, years later, that light always wins over darkness.

At the age of five, there is no tangible evidence to prove what your past was like at all. This leads to a lifetime of self-doubt, a lack of confidence, self-destructiveness in some, and a total mistrust of anyone in authority, including work bosses. The inability to know what happened to you pulls you apart from the inside. One instinctively searches themselves for answers. What have I done wrong? Where have I been? Truth and untruth become impossible to separate from each other. A disjointed thought process has been programmed into you, and there is a void where normal thoughts and feelings were once housed.

If there is something that will knock a child's confidence for life, it is being spoon-fed a catalogue of lies, being calculatedly steered towards feelings of rejection, purposefully separated from siblings – leading to maximum instability in that moment – and most of all, being denied the unconditional love that can only come from family. But they couldn't take away my inner fire, my inner passion, my innate inner strength, my innate inner humour and my innate inner caring. They couldn't beat me because I was, and still am, me.

The care home I went to was in Castlecroft in the district of Wolverhampton. It was a big place with a rough tarmac driveway and lots of pine trees. There were two gates, a wrought-iron pedestrian one and a large double one. The double gates were usually closed – especially if the kids were outside – and would be used to allow deliveries of food, supplies and new orphans. The oppressive building was surrounded by huge walls –

walls which I hope someone has knocked down now and tracked into the dust. I haven't been able to muster up the strength to go back to look.

The home housed both boys and girls, and they were separated into different dormitories. There was no privacy at all, meaning that it was impossible to have any time away from the other residents. There was a television room, which was staffed by so-called carers who just stood and watched you like prison guards. If you talked, slouched, breathed or moved in any way, you were sent into the reading room to sit alone facing the wall. And if you continued to be a child and make noise, your next destination would be the broom cupboard, though only after you'd had the slipper or the belt to your backside – I think they got off on it. We called any cupboard 'The Broom Cupboard', though some were worse than others.

On occasion you got slaps and sometimes full-on punches from members of staff, both male and female. But that was normal, and you had to be grateful that that was all you got. The reading room was just another big communal room with tables and chairs, where you had to sit and read quietly under constant surveillance of a carer. And, of course, just like the television room, there was no slouching, talking or breathing.

Further down the main corridor, there was a big communal dining room – which was attached to the kitchens – and two small meeting rooms, where some kids met their parents on visits all under close supervision. No one was left alone in there. I went to both rooms many times to be interviewed by social workers, and there was always a third party individual watching. I never had a visit from any member of family, but was sometimes introduced to prospective foster parents. There was a staff room even further down the corridor, but we dared not look in its direction, let alone enter it. We were just viewed as criminals, who would pinch anything that wasn't nailed down and attack the staff with anything we could get hold of and use as a weapon.

Shortly after being taken into this care home, I received a horrific injury to my forehead. It put me in hospital, and I had stitches and butterfly stitches as a result. I still bear deep scars on my forehead as proof of this occurrence. The object that caused this injury was a heavy metal ashtray in the shape of a hand, with the palm being used for ash. The reason I know this ashtray was the cause of my injury is because I was told by people I trusted: the other children, who saw the ashtray bloodstained with bits of my forehead attached to its cold metal fingers.

This ashtray was in the staffroom, and I had seen it before on the table through the open door of the room. We were not allowed in the staffroom, and, to my knowledge, I had never been in there. We did not dare to break the rules, and, besides, the members of staff were constantly watching us. We had to put our hand up and ask if we wanted to go to the toilet, and more often than not we would be refused and then beaten for wetting ourselves. If we went to the bathroom we would be escorted and sometimes watched while we urinated or sat on the toilet. Having control over you seemed paramount to them – the indignity you suffered did not matter to them at all. Looking wasn't all they did, but I don't think it's necessary to expose the reader to details of that.

The only way for me to have been in there is if a member of staff had taken me in. Perhaps because I was a fresh, new, young, little boy – someone different. I could not have got in there by any other means, and I know that because I was a prisoner there for long enough to know the rules well.

Why was an attempt made on my life? Why would this occurrence have been brushed under the table as an accident? Who walked in to the staffroom? It is very likely that I had disturbed someone that was themselves extremely disturbed. This person probably smashed the ashtray into my forehead in an attempt to create a diversion – to cover up what was being done to me. Fortunately, I have no memory of the events leading up to this incident, and I hope that I never will.

Though there are of course many other incidents I do remember that are branded into my mind. However much I try, I cannot erase them. When things like this happen, you blame yourself, even though you do realise that none of it was of your doing. Despite this, I am still alive and by living, in a way, I have won. Though I cannot deny that there were occasions where the thought of a noose was more inviting than the thought of living. I could see myself lifeless and swinging… I wanted to be with my mummy and daddy again.

The people that witness or even suspect that these events are happening should speak up straight away, no matter how high up the rank of the perpetrator. When the eyes of a witness see the truth, they should not allow the rank of the perpetrator to dissuade them from reporting it, because by not speaking up the observer becomes as guilty as the perpetrator. Policies and procedures should be re-written to enforce this, and regular unannounced audits of these systems should take place at least monthly and feedback should be regularly sought. Procedures should relate to the actual occurrences on-site, and people should be talked to in order to gauge what works and what doesn't. Familiarity breeds contempt, so the auditors need to be different each time. People need to remember that auditing is not a judgement of the people, it is a judgement of the system.

By not speaking up, it is as though the witness almost sees the abuse as acceptable. They are condoning the abuser's actions, and compounding the problem by letting them carry on unchecked. Too many people are afraid to challenge their peers. There is almost a psychological barrier for abusers, and it prevents them from even worrying about getting caught. And the sad truth is they get away with it, and then they get bolder. People continue to turn a blind eye instead of blowing the whistle on these perverts, and never think to draw attention to the fact that someone is not quite acting right or that they are deviating from a recognised work pattern.

People in general, both in and out of the care system, should be more vigilant in spotting and reporting such incidents. If the people they tell cover it up, then they should – if they are to live up to their name as a carer – take it higher up. And if the people in the higher positions don't take things forward, then they should tell others and try to make noise.

The kids themselves have the same problem. If they tell they get ridiculed, have their mouth washed out with soap and end up getting a beating for telling the truth. Mostly they don't know what's happening or why – they are called liars for even suggesting that something has happened to them. For some of them it is just the norm, it's what happens – it is what has always happened to them.

It's a case of: 'How dare you question my authority? Do you realise who I am? Do you realise what an impertinent, horrible little wretch of a child you are?'

Due to this type of attitude, us kids wouldn't tell the members of staff anything. We knew that if we did it would all too readily be turned back on us as though it was all our fault for leading staff on – or for letting the older kids do what they liked to us. Predictably, like with so many things that I still see prevalent in life today, the victim more often than not would become the perpetrator, and the whistle-blower would become the victim. So with that in mind at such a young age, we kept it all to ourselves. They couldn't handle the truth anyway – they couldn't accept their own moral failings. We formed alliances among ourselves, just as anyone would when faced with such an adverse situation. We had to rely on ourselves, because the staff wouldn't help us. We weren't their kids so why should they care about us? It was just a job to them.

But in a way we *were* their kids, we were our country's kids, and the duty of care lies with every citizen of this country. We all owe it to our own moralities to care and look after young, vulnerable people – whatever their race, creed, abilities, background or circumstances. The kids that are mentally and physically challenged, the refugees, the victims of natural disasters from foreign countries – if they are in our country, we have a duty to give them the best care possible. They are our future assets, but invariably we turn them into permanent drains on the public purse by not giving them the best care available at a young age. It's not the failing of aftercare from the age of 18 years old, it's the failing of pre-care from before the age of 18 years old that counts. It is important to help people when they are young.

The only questions to be asked are: 'Have you ever been in a disadvantaged situation?' and 'Have any of these things ever affected you personally?'

Ask, and hear it from the horse's mouth. And don't just listen, discuss and learn from those that have seen it first-hand and have lived it. Don't be one of those people who only looks inward, from afar, in a glass house, with rose-tinted spectacles. It's not right.

One of the main things I remember about being brought up in council care homes was the public sector, militant, robot-like lifestyle, and the accompanying discipline – so cold and unfeeling. We were children, but they treated us like hardened criminals. That is not to say that I do not have the utmost respect for people that work in the service, but I'm speaking from a childhood perspective. There of course had to be a certain structure for the care home to function, so that all of the kids could be fed and washed, and the cleaning could be done. It was a 24 hours a day, 365 days per year operation. But it felt like a factory/production line. We needed discipline, but certainly not the harsh, unfeeling discipline that was dealt out to us by controlling and unemotional jobsworths.

These people, these so-called carers, these do-gooder social workers who were no doubt privileged, and assumed it was their God-given right to control frightened, confused, vulnerable and mentally ill children. These people who were produced like machines, who had suspicion bred into them – and caring bred out of them – would ask such personal and demeaning questions in attempts to make themselves appear human to us children. Questions like 'Did they touch you?' and 'What did they ask you to do?'

It was always these generic, 'yes or no', tick-the-box questions – it was impossible for them to deviate from their forms. This behaviour was too militant-like, and was almost reminiscent of WW2. Us kids, at the age of ten, had been through more hurt than most people receive in a lifetime. We were streetwise and on the ball, and we had natural senses and inbuilt awareness. We were alive, we were kids, we were human beings. We related to each other, we emphasised with each other, cared and looked out for each other – but we couldn't always protect ourselves from the perverse staff and sometimes the older kids, who would prey on some of us like predators. Some kids are cruel: it was us and them – the predators – from the start.

For us, caring for each other was inherent – we had a bond that couldn't be broken. We would lie to the staff and tell them nothing; we just stuck together and got on with life as best we could. We saw telling as grassing, and it was an unwritten rule that whatever happens you don't grass – no matter how intolerable life becomes and however much you want to say yes and not no during those form-filling, box-ticking exercises. Those paper systems did not always work in every situation, and the carers needed to realise that they were dealing with our lives and not just pieces of paper. Trying to relate to people and emphasise with them is more important than simple yes or no answers. It was their lack of caring, their inability to recognise pain in kids, their lack of will, skills and proper training that stopped us from being helped.

You could, quite literally, eat your dinner off the floor without fear of contamination. Though you would undoubtedly taste bleach or Dettol. I am still to this day placed back into that harsh environment – the dormitory beds and linoleum floors – when my olfactory system picks up the smell of bleach, Dettol, Jeyes Fluid or urine. The windows were cleaned constantly, and there was always at least one covered with Windowlene at any time. People would always be cutting the grass, trimming hedges, working in the kitchens and doing just general D.I.Y. The place was a hive of activity, and so you never got any 'me' time – you were theirs, you belonged to them. They had your heart and soul and they knew you knew it. You were owned and controlled, not loved and nurtured.

We had no identities at all. We only had one birthday, and I really mean one birthday in the sense that all of us children, boys and girls alike, had one collective birthday. It sounds strange, but due to this I didn't even know when my real birthday was. That was demoralising and damaging, I can tell you. One had no possessions whatsoever. No toys, and no clothing other than pyjamas, a school uniform, and stuff to wear after school, all of which miraculously appeared on the chair next to your metal frame bed. We were only given hand-me-downs – none of which fitted, and all of which made us stand out as target practice for the bastard kids.

One year – though this may have happened at other times as well – we got toys for Christmas. People in suits came around, probably from charities or the government, gleefully slapping themselves on the back. The patronising, aloof prats were so up themselves, so detached from reality, that they didn't want to see the truth of our situation. So long as they got their mugshots in the local newspaper, they were happy. They wouldn't have seen the truth if it jumped up and bit them in the ass, or if it was written in six-foot-high neon letters. Ironically, they probably claimed that they were the ones that were looking after us. All from a distance, of course. So long as we were behind closed doors and not in their back yards – so that they could just come and see us at the zoo when they felt the need – then the treatment we received was okay with them. But their treatment of us hurt – getting scraps in the form of toys and then getting them snatched back almost immediately afterwards. I'm sure lots of them had false teeth, just so they could take them out before they spoke to save lying through them.

We stood in a line on the cold tiled floor and each received a toy. I received a lovely black and white panda. It was only about a foot tall, and it was second hand. I remember it so clearly – I loved it. I held it so tight, but I was no match for the strong arms of the care staff that pried it away from me once the people in suits had gone. The care staff put it in a big trunk, ready to be given out again when the next lot of high profile visitors wanted something to patronisingly give out. It sounds silly, but I still think about my panda to this day. You would think that even those aloof dummies would realise they were giving out the same toys over and over again. I suppose it's only the blind that can see, and, as Bob Marley said, 'some people are so poor that all they have is money.'

On one side of my dormitory bed, there was a small square table, which was a platform for a lamp and a bible, and on the other side there was a wooden chair, where my school uniform would miraculously appear, all washed and pressed, every day after my cold bath. The metal bed frames squeaked, and each of the uncomfortable mattresses had a protective rubber covering in case of bedwetting.

There was a crucifix above each bed, and you had to pray every night before you went to sleep. That is, if you could sleep. If the itchy woollen blankets and sweaty piss-liner didn't keep you awake, then the fear of hearing a bed squeak would. You were on guard all night, asking yourself if you would be next. Kids would wake up screaming all of the time, their damaged minds giving them flashbacks of earlier traumas and their fragile bodies being unable to fight back. But no one would ever come to help them, no one would take any notice of the shouts and screams, it was just a part of the whole regime. My nightmares were of a strapped-down man with outstretched arms beckoning for me to come nearer, whilst looking straight into my eyes and screaming in pain. Nightmares sometimes became very real, and it was hauntingly terrifying when you heard the words of an adult saying, 'There's a good boy. Just be quiet and lay still, I'm not going to hurt you.' And then getting your face licked and breathed on while being subject to roaming hands. No questions on their forms mentioned those situations.

The girls' dormitories were the same, and they told us similar stories. I'll never understand why it was allowed to go on so blatantly. I have read books and I have spoken to other orphans, and we cannot all be wrong – we cannot all be so far off the mark. The authorities should listen to the same notes being sung by so many; the evidence is overwhelming on all counts with no deviations. If you want to question two people, you separate them and ask them each the same questions. If their answers differ too much, then someone is lying. The police have got thousands of people from multiple decades all banging the same drum, all to the same beat, all with no deviations, and they are ignoring all of them. Who is wrong? WHO IS WRONG!!?

Would any sane person let their children or their relatives' children go through such events – allowing them to be physically and mentally tortured, never knowing when or if it will ever stop? Kids at the home self-harmed, cutting their legs, forearms and even their torsos in a cry for help. Witnessing kids do this is just as damaging to the other children. Then, when they grow older, they just end up doing to others what was done to them when they were younger. There was no escape from the violence for us. The people who ignored it are just as guilty as those that inflicted it, such as the satanic Mrs Davenport. But in the end we survived, we will tell our stories and through that we shall win.

We hated the regime, we hated the cold, cold discipline, and we hated the early morning cold baths with multiple occupants at once. Some children even deliberately peed or even defecated in the cold water as acts of defiance. We hated being made to sweep the yard and driveway in the cold of mid-winter while wearing short-sleeved shirts and shorts. We couldn't handle the adult-sized, hard brooms that gave us blisters. We couldn't cope with the borstal type regime. We needed care, love, hope and most of all to feel a sense of belonging. We didn't just want our families, we needed them. We hated the beatings, and we hated being locked in the outhouse overnight. If it wasn't freezing, we would be locked in the broom cupboard instead. The cruel, inhumane carers knew that there wasn't even enough room to sit down to rest. And yes, of course, the next morning before school, we were subjected to the routine of having a cold bath and sweeping up pine needles from the rough tarmac driveway. Being locked in the broom cupboard was bad enough, but it became even worse when you heard footsteps in the corridor at night, and wondered what was going to happen when the door opened? *What now? Why? Please, God no.*

After the already spotless yard had been swept, it was time for breakfast. It was a chance to be demeaned, dehumanised and demoralised even further, having to face the indignity of eating cheap processed slop off of plastic plates. Yes, plastic plates and plastic cutlery – it was as though we were in for mass murder. Was there no level they were unwilling to stoop below in order to break us kids? Even my dog Jess has a ceramic bowl, as I wouldn't give her a plastic one to eat out of. And besides, if I did, she'd probably chew it in defiance. They left us with dead eyes throughout our lives, mechanically destroying and dissecting any sense of belonging, and tearing the memories out of our tiny fragile bodies.

Before breakfast we had to set the table with the plastic plates. If a piece of bendy plastic cutlery was out of alignment or a plastic plate or side-plate didn't line up, both down and across the table, then the table would have to be re-set by crying, frightened children. Personally and fortunately, I couldn't remember what life before care was like during that period – so having to behave in such a way was all I knew. Once the table was set, we would dish out the inedible slop, and then wait for Mrs Davenport to sit down at the head of the table. We would stand behind our chairs, arms at our sides and eyes looking straight ahead, and then Mrs Davenport would start to say grace. We would automatically clasp our hands in front of ourselves, and our heads would robotically look down. After grace was said, we were allowed the indignity of listening to Mrs Davenport's freakishly controlling German accent as she said, 'You may now be seated.'

We sat and then had to wait until we were told that we could eat. We could not reach for anything, even if it was right next to us. It was always, 'Please may you pass me the salt?' We could not speak to each other unless we were asking for something to be passed, or asking to go to the toilet. I saw children pee and sometimes defecate themselves after having their request to leave the table refused by Mrs Davenport. This, I believe, was the most damaging and demeaning part of it all. To be denied the right to go to the toilet is immoral. Making someone urinate or defecate themselves is one thing to which no human being should stoop so low, but to then make them eat, along with the rest of the children, while the smell of their faeces wafts around, is quite another level of depravity. We would be retching whilst trying to eat, with the smell of faeces wafting through the air. For those former carers to be able to walk upright in society, knowing things like this happened, makes no sense to me. Someone somewhere should have alerted the outside world to such events. They were physical events, visible to all in attendance – but they were treated as if they were invisible or unworthy of mentioning. People knew and said nothing. If they read this book and tell the truth now, then I will gladly accept their admittance.

Slop finished, the plates would be washed up by us kids and put away. I was regularly asked to put away the lovely plastic cutlery. Mrs Davenport would open the big flat drawer, and I would have to put the cutlery into a certain design, fanning out spoons, knives and forks in various patterns. She would always have a frightened pupil beside her, a new kid or someone she had it in for. After I finished she would say, 'Isn't it beautiful, Keith?' and then slam the drawer shut, re-open it and force the new kid to arrange the jumbled mess of plastic cutlery into the same pattern I had put it in. The poor child would receive countless blows and insults because of their inability to recreate what I had done. This affected me like it did the victim. Once I tried to help the victim, and I say once as I never ever dared to do it again. To this day I am reluctant to help others, but my innate good nature helps me to overcome the fear that Mrs Davenport instilled in me. You see, I'm still scared of her now – she still traumatises me. I see her face, I hear her voice, and I remember all – not just some – of the beatings dished out by her. My human rights were violated in every way imaginable. Hers an utterly depraved mind. It amazes me that that woman was a mother herself – and I'm sure some of the male staff must have been fathers too. I wouldn't let any of them keep a rat.

We went to school only to be traumatised some more. The ordinary school kids hated us, and we were picked on relentlessly. Like myself, the other orphans had been through mental torture, physical beatings, and sexual abuse from carers and other residents. Those kids were tough.

We suffered multiple mental and physical knocks from the ordinary school kids, but we would never allow ourselves to be broken. Usually the perpetrators became victims through our self-defence, but never would they be told off – it was always the child from the orphanage that would be given detention and a clip around the ear. More often than not the teacher would experience our wrath, and most likely think twice about how to handle the next incident.

The girls were the toughest though, and they would stick together like glue. They not only punched like the lads, but they would scratch, pinch and kick in ways that us boys couldn't hope to match. They were bigger, stronger and faster than us – they were calculating and impossible to beat. There weren't as many of them as there were of us, but thank God they were on our side. They, like us wouldn't tell on others or grass, but they would plot and initiate plans of revenge. They had good verbal skills, something us lads just didn't have.

There has been, I'm sure, great improvement in the care system in recent years, and in light of complaints and accusations from various people, I would like to clarify that I am talking about the 1960s and 1970s here. Things have since changed and moved on, and I pray that these changes have been enforced. I pray that no child will ever suffer again in the ways that I did. I also consider this book to be about control in general, and the ways people have it over each other.

After the age of ten or eleven, I could and did look after myself – fearing nothing and no-one. I never initiated any kind of hostility, and am still a very passive person today, but I could defend myself to the nth degree. I had fists, feet, knees, elbows, nails and even teeth at my disposal, and I deployed whatever I needed to win. Sometimes I'd even have to pick things up to defend myself. However, if I was outnumbered, I would run, beg, grovel cowardly or just take a beating, only to pick them off one by one later on. I never gave mercy, and because of this I never lost again. After a while even the kids in the upper years of school stopped bothering me. If you fed one a piece of their bitten-off ear, they would tell others and then all of them would just leave you alone.

Fortunately, I never received one of those Bic pen ink tattoos. Most of the kids had them, both boys and girls, and the choices available were 'breathtakingly awesome' awesome - from the fingers to the forearm it was:

Fingers

- Right Hand – LOVE   - Left Hand – HATE
- Right Hand – MUM †   - Left Hand – DAD †
- Right Hand – RIP †   - Left Hand – MUM †
- Right Hand - RIP †   - Left Hand – DAD †

Knuckles

- You had a choice of Dots or Stars

Wrists

- You Could have a dotted line around your wrist
- You could have a dotted line with 'Cut Here'

Forearms

So really, the combinations of crudely executed tattoos you could have was endless. You'd place your arm on the table, dip the needle into the ink, and keep pricking your skin. One thing I have to say in the kids who did it's favour: they put a match under the needle to sterilise it.

Every now and then one us would be taken away to stay with a foster family. For some kids it worked out well and we never saw them again; we prayed they would be happy with their new family. At least we thought they'd gone to a family – we were never really told. It was like the film *The Great Escape*: it was impossible to know if they had escaped for sure, or if they'd simply been taken out of the frying pan and put into the fire. I really do hope that all of the kids found good homes with good people, and subsequently led good and happy lives.

Every now and then a day would come when I'd find my stuff packed, and a staff member would say to me, 'Keith, can you come with me?' I'd be taken into one of the small meeting rooms and introduced to my new foster parents. They'd sign some paperwork and then I'd have to go with them in the car to wherever they lived. Never would I know in advance where I was going, how long I'd be with them or what the people were like.

Some of them were nice and some were old-fashioned and horrible – though I don't doubt that they had good intentions. With every new school I'd receive the same old questions, the same old hostility and same messed-up month of education. Some of the normal kids at school would get bloody noses for pushing their luck when attempting to bully me, or for calling me the 'new bastard kid'. And, of course, for doing so I would get the blame and receive detention, the cane or have to stand in the corner of the classroom. Though it was them who picked fights, it was always me that got the blame. I often wondered if they would get the blame if they won the fights, but I think the answer to that is obvious... No normal kid was ever to blame, no member of staff from the home was ever to blame, and it was always the orphan kid that lost.

The foster parents would always eventually drop me back off at the home. Without being too cynical, I'm sure most of them took in orphans just so they could brag about how pious and upstanding they were at the golf club, church socials and coffee mornings. But the truth is, both from my viewpoint as a child and an adult, that such actions just mess up a kid's life.

I now know that some foster parents did this part-time and probably had good intentions, thinking they were either helping the child, helping the children's home or both, but I just saw it as disruption. They built your hopes up and then dropped you like a stone, making your guts hurt and your head explode. Why didn't they just treat us like normal human beings and say, 'Keith, Mr and Mrs X would like you to stay with them for a fortnight, is that okay? You would come back here afterwards?' Not just pick you up and drop you off, leaving you totally shocked and disorientated, but full of hope at the same time.

We hated the home and we hated the staff, but the other kids at the home were like extended family. We loved each other like brothers and sisters, because we grew up together, we related with each other and we had all been through the same mill. There was an unspoken code and we all always knew what was happening, even though we were only kids. We were survivors, and we knew that together we could win both in the home and at school.

I wouldn't comply with anybody's views or any rules. The other children picked the fat kid instead of me for football, because I would pull shirts, push, kick, bite and pick the ball up with my own hands; anything to get the ball into my own team's goal. It wasn't that the other kids at school didn't like me, because I was quite popular, it was just that I wouldn't comply with anyone else's rules. I saw games as a form of control, and I saw that the rules were there to be broken in order to leave the teacher with no control. I was no team player, I was me. This resulted in the teachers even refusing to accept me onto their teams, and I was often made to run around the pitch for the duration of the game. Sometimes I'd do cross-country running, which I loved, because it gave me some escapism and freedom, and other times I'd just go off for a smoke with my packet of No. 6 and refuse to do any exercise. The phrase 'stubborn as a mule' doesn't even cover how bad I was.

Although it wasn't all bad all of the time. We would go to the swimming baths in Wolverhampton on Saturday mornings, like I did with my brothers, and we also went to the Saturday matinee in the same Odeon cinema I went to when I was younger. Like before, the cinema would show *The Lone Ranger Rides Again* and *Champion the Wonder Horse*, but not *Flash Gordon*. I didn't like it anyhow. We got the bus from outside the home with a member of staff and off we went.

There were also trips to the seaside, but not so many. They were just in the summer holidays, I think. We would go off in the minibus to places like Rhyl, Skegness and even Land's End. Sometimes we would camp and other times stay in hostels and bed & breakfast boarding houses. So things weren't all bad all of the time. We only generally stayed for one night, but that was enough for us – it was just good to get out of the home. We would be under constant supervision – everything but the razor wire, the balls and chains and orange overalls – but it was worth it just to be a way.

We went out to play on the weekends, walking unaccompanied for miles down the canal and in the woods, where we'd make swings, dens and do what kids do. We always stuck together as a group, we always hung back for the tired, and we always looked out for each other.

Normal children didn't mix with us, they didn't come near us at all, and if they were with their parents then we got looks of disdain from them. The parents would motion for us to stay away, turning their backs on us like ewes corralling their lambs to safety. We were well used to this sort of behaviour on account of our situation – we already felt unwanted – and so we paid no heed to them. We just went about our business of being outside and free for a few hours. Our haircuts and our clothes gave away where we were from. All our clothes were ill-fitting hand-me-downs, and, of course, we always had plastic jelly sandals that were too small and made us walk with discomfort.

There was little playing when we got back to the home – there was playing cards, chess and draughts and that was our lot. And if we didn't play those in silence, there would be a trip to the broom cupboard. I was quite good at chess, but was never let into the chess club at school – their loss, I reckon. Again, it was that aloof mentality. I wasn't from the right class to be allowed to play chess, even though I was good and strategic. We could also sew or knit – I didn't like either – but if I had to, I would sew by hand with no machines. The sewing area is probably where the expert tattooists got their needles from. We generally made cushions, sometimes felt animals – I think we often made squirrels – but we never saw what we made in the home. I don't really know what happened to the cushions or the squirrels. I was rubbish at sewing, because I was just too gawky and clumsy, but it did help pass the time. Though to be honest, it was still boring and about as much use to a young boy as tits on a fish.

The consequences of being brought up in care – being constantly moved from pillar to post and having multiple schools – follow you throughout your life. You make friends and they want to know about your past, but you cannot tell them, because they always say, 'Oh, what a shame', 'That must have been awful for you' and 'What was it like?', among other controlling, inquisitive, negative, demeaning things.

I for one do not want to relive my past by having it brought up. It hurts. It is so painful that it fills my eyes with tears every time I so much as momentarily think about it. I don't blame people for asking as it's human nature, but some twist their questions into a way of controlling you. They tell others, and discuss and dissect your story, and you always end up on the side-lines – nothing more than a topic for debate. So you don't tell them anything, and like a Ferris Wheel the game of cat and mouse goes around and around. They of course stereotype you as a troublemaker, a thief and a liar, and all because they are afraid and ignorant. People don't seem to be able to get past that roadblock when you tell them you are in care, or, when you are older, that you've been in care. To me it is quite strange, because to me I am normal. Being brought up in a care home was all I knew, I'd forgotten my brothers and parents and didn't really know if they existed. I knew no other life as such.

People question, re-question and examine every sentence of a child that's been brought up in care, and compare and contrast it with the benchmark demeanour of a child that's been brought up in a normal family home environment. You are never accepted, or indeed deemed acceptable, and so you have to keep your past a secret, you have to be on your guard, and you have to keep your cards very close to your chest at all times. You have to try to emulate someone you are very much not in order to resemble a stereotypical child.

I thought for many years that I had really had a very privileged upbringing, being brought up in council care, but I was of course very wrong. I really didn't know any different as council care was all I had ever known. Also, I thought I was very privileged in having all the other residents as brothers and sisters, and the members of staff as aunts and uncles. Who else had such a large caring family? The fact that care homes made you grow up fast and made you tough was something else I liked, but I was still a young boy, and was and still am messed up. Eventually I realised that being brought up in council care was a tragedy and not something to be proud of at all. I also realised in time that everything about being brought up in those unfeeling places was wrong; the imposing, oppressive buildings were really just extents of what laid within.

The bad treatment of orphans – who needed nothing more than a safe harbour to dock in – perpetrated by some of these care homes surely could not have been accidental. There did of course need to be some sort of structural, institutionalised discipline – but why so harsh? And why was such behaviour accepted, and deemed acceptable, by bystanders who witnessed what occurred? Quite frankly, that's why they got away with it – no one talks about what happened or tries to expose it. The 'stiff upper-lip' attitude prevails and the fingers in ears, 'I am not listening', attitude... Certain occurrences are safely fenced off by people's attitudes, and compounded and endorsed by their ignorance.

The things that occurred stayed entombed within the walls of the institutions, perhaps because the members of staff wouldn't dare challenge their peers. But surely the care homes couldn't have all been the same throughout the country, surely they couldn't have all adopted the same ignorant, obstinate type of attitude? I understand that what happened was isolated, and I understand that whichever particular individuals managed those individual localised homes had great influences on them. I just hope that they were not all like the satanic Mrs Davenport and her band of villains. Though perhaps 'villains' is too good a word, and perhaps villains shouldn't be typecast or stereotyped as faceless, gutless people that prey on young children under the cloak of an upstanding position – a position where they have power over their victims. It is the aloof, 'we are the kings of the castle' mentality, which is in some ways reminiscent of the still prevalent class system. It is control. It is the weak-minded putting themselves in positions of power, and the sick and the depraved being allowed to prevail and go about their perverse, chameleonic trade unnoticed.

There are of course people that have blown the whistle on others, whether it be in this sort of situation or another, mostly in government-run establishments.

They get surrounded, suspended, sieged and demoralised. They become outcasts and their opinions are swept under the table like rubbish. These are people that have known what they were up against before they dared to challenge the forces, the NHS, the care homes or whatever. These are people that knew they would be discredited and pulled down, and as a result of this, meticulously kept years of diaries, of times, dates and facts, of unscrupulous occurrences, and still they soldier on. They are people that should be held in high regard, but instead get the 'lock them outside the city walls and let no man feed them or offer them shelter' attitude.

'How dare they? How damned impertinent of them to question us?' Well, they are not impertinent at all, they are our soldiers, our nurses, our police, our patients, our elderly and our children, and they are simply displaying a duty of care that we should all demonstrate towards each other. They are people that do speak up when procedures are not followed. They speak out when it is proven beyond all reasonable doubt that protocol has not been followed or rules have been bent – or broken entirely. Even when some people are faced with damming concrete evidence, they spin it, twist it and turn it in such a way as to make it acceptable for them to deny the charges put to them. This is why people get away with things, because the whole country, under the ruling of a law – made by some magistrate – is backing them up by not listening to the victims' voices, however young, however mentally ill and however old they are. No matter how much they have served our great country in their chosen vocation or service. We have a duty of care as a nation to expose the rotten apples. Just because children get taken into care it doesn't mean they are somehow the dregs of society, and it doesn't mean they are low hanging fruit, left to be picked freely by the individuals lacking any morals without consequences. And I have more news: the Earth is not flat, it is spherical, so deal with it and move on.

Occasionally, throughout my life, I've been asked by people how I coped, and indeed how I still do. Well, I can tell you. I sit or stand and I imagine I'm a big immovable tree standing at the head of a valley, looking down at the green fields and forest below me. Next to me on my right is a waterfall, and I can see a silver, meandering thread of water working its way down the green valley. Sometimes there are sheep and lambs, and sometimes there are cows with their calves and walkers with their dogs. Sometimes there is only the landscape. As I breathe in the tree sways backwards, and as I breathe out the tree sways forward, with the wind filling my canopy. I breathe in the air, allowing it to go right down my trunk and into my roots. This is where the good feelings go and the bad expire. This technique must have been taught to me as a child – most likely by some ex-carer that was a remnant of the late 60s 'flower power' movement. Nevertheless, no matter when or where I acquired this technique, it has always stayed with me and it has always helped me. I am thankful for the ability to become a tree in times of need. It works for me, and if it isn't broken then don't fix it – a great motto.

Again, I would like to state that I hope this script brings strength, inspiration and peace to others. I do know that things have since changed, I do know that policies and procedures have been brought in and implemented, and I also know that it is really difficult to change entrenched mind-sets and human behavioural traits. I know in my heart that this wasn't countrywide, but it did happen, and the children's voices should have been heard then, at the time, and not 50 years after the mental torment elapsed. But even then, back in the 1960s and 1970s, they must have understood that their actions would create a future demand for long-term care, and that it would lead to long-term social injustice, long-term deprivation and long-term hurt. There can be no justification for their unacceptable treatment of innocent children, incarcerating them in so-called care homes.

Of course, this treatment is visible through the people that have been subjected to such barrages of abuse. It shines like a lighthouse, etched into their sad eyes, voice, choice of words, gait and posture, and it stays with them for the rest of their life. I know as a result of experiencing this anomaly of family life that I can walk into a café or a bar and instantly recognise this void in others. I can see that they've been brought up in one institution or another from a young age. I can see it in their eyes, recognise it in their gaze, and observe a void in their posture. They in turn recognise it in me and we both say nothing. I have nothing but the utmost respect for this person, this total stranger whose inner soul I feel I know. All of us are deconstructed in the same way: once we were different and individuals, but now that they've taken apart and reassembled us, we are the same as all the others. These people, like myself, have an air of beaten-ness about them, and they are also unassuming. It is a quality of knowing that the average person does not acquire until they have experienced a lifetime full of hurt, bereavement and knockbacks. These people have had the edges knocked off of them long, long ago and to some tune.

The George Inn

I was in and out of more schools, foster homes, and care homes than I can count. I had more social workers and carers than I can remember, but I do remember the last one very clearly, a woman about to retire called Mrs Valerie Stena. Mrs Stena was friends with my soon-to-be foster parents. Apparently, I was advertised in the Lichfield Mercury newspaper – which I found a little bit insulting – but I suppose in hindsight there wasn't much else they could have done in those days with no computers. Nevertheless, it was still almost like being held in comparison to a dog for sale. I would love to have seen that advertisement if it at all existed, just so I could transcribe it and put it into this book. Maybe it read 'non-compliant, uncontrollable feral child for sale, rent or other' – like in the film *Oliver*, when Mr Bumble the beadle paraded the workhouse boy Oliver through the town in an attempt to get rid of him.

One Boy,
Boy for Sale,
He's going cheap,
How much then?
Only seven guineas.
How Much?
That or thereabouts
Small boy…
Rather pale…

From lack of sleep.

Feed him gruel dinners.

Stop him getting stout…

One thing I can say in my new foster parents' favour is that my foster mother took me to get my feet measured, and subsequently bought me some shoes that fitted. I had been wearing an ill-fitting pair of jelly sandals for years, which I was glad to bin. I remember the cobbler in the shoe shop measuring my feet and looking shocked when he saw the state of them. He took my foster mother to one side to have a quiet word with her – you know when someone speaks about you as though you are not present – and my foster mother explained to him that I was a foster child, and that the state of my feet was not of her doing. Others in the shop were brought over to marvel at my scrunched up toes. My toes still fold over each other today, each of them is bent, and sometimes in cold or really warm weather they hurt. The sweat makes them blister and abrade, and the cold brings out the rheumatism – a painful gout-like feeling.

I knew no different, but how on Earth did schoolteachers, carers and general adults not notice my feet, just overlooking them completely? And how on Earth did they get away with not noticing and turning a blind eye? They were just as complicit in the act as those that had given me the sandals. It wasn't as though there were no other tell-tale signs; my clothes didn't fit, with my shirt sleeves and trousers being too short – I was a big lad for my age – and my hair was a mop. Ever since the day when I got those new shoes, I have polished the life out of every subsequent pair I have had. And a good job too, because I didn't get a lot of anything from my new foster parents. They certainly gave me no love, care or good treatment. Although I did get one thing, and plenty of it: work.

I would also like to add at this point, before I go deeper into talking about my last pair of foster parents, that I'd previously had foster parents who lived in a big detached house just outside of Lichfield. I only know this location because I drove past the house later in life and recognised it. I pulled over, walked back, and yes, it was the house. Its occupants, my former foster parents, Mr and Mrs Hood, were controlling also. Do these people all come from the same mould? Do they just have a factory where they produce these mentally detached people?

Mr and Mrs Hood handed me back after they realised I was left-handed, which defies all my sense of logic. Mr Hood used to sit me at the table with writing paper in front of me, a pen in my right hand and my left arm strapped down to the back of the chair. However much I try, I cannot figure out why he did this to a child. My arm must have been covered in bruises from the strap, and the rest of my body too from being prodded and goaded into writing with my right hand. He would tell me how stupid I was, and I'd have to endure countless slaps and punches. Mr and Mrs Hood had a son and a daughter of their own, but they didn't treat them like they treated me. I was just a bastard kid for them to bully and belittle. But they didn't really count on the fact that I had been through a lot worse than they could dish out, they also didn't count on the fact that I could hit back, and they certainly didn't envisage getting overwhelmed by a scrawny bastard kid.

Were they all just so mentally detached? Was I just there as a freak show, as entertainment for the whole blooming family? I remember being treated as such regularly, it's welded into the inside of my skull as a really bad nightmare and I can't remove it or even begin to comprehend why anyone would treat any living soul in such a way; people wouldn't treat animals as badly as I was treated. It was pure control again, and I'm sure they were purely devoid of human emotions.

Are these people not vetted? Are these people not monitored? Are the bruises on the child not seen? Are the bruises, gait and demeanour of the child even taken into consideration on assessments, or reported or acted upon?

Ah, well, you see, the generic form does it all – it's just the same old story. The workers would stick to generic form-ticking exercises featuring the generic questions, with them not allowing themselves to deviate once. Us kids were just treated as bits of paper. But we weren't – and it was cold, unfeeling and immoral to think of us as such.

Does that ticked form prevent me from waking up at night, still to this day, thinking that my arm has been tied down? If there is no human intervention in these situations, if people remain emotionally detached from the lives of others, then nothing will ever progress and nothing will ever move forward. Everything is probably done remotely by phone and computer now, meaning that the form gives even less leeway with regards to the information that is inputted. Does just the pure fact that you have ticked a box on a form mean everything alright? I think these forms must be like something out of the *Nutcracker*; they come alive at night, when no one is looking, and do stuff that we are unaware of.

And now I lead you on to the next set of sadistic lunatics who graced my life – the next pair of control freaks.

My new foster parents – who would become my longest lasting and final ones – were David and Rosemary Burton. They lived in a little hamlet called Elmhurst, near Lichfield. David worked for a local land-owner on a farm – it was mainly arable with some beef – and Rose worked in a tobacconist's in Lichfield. They were both about 40 years old and seemed to be quite normal, or as best as I could judge – I was only 13. They lived in a three-bedroom bungalow that was rented from the owner of the estate, who David worked for.

There was a kitchen cum dining room cum living room, a large lounge that was only used to house two large freezers, three bedrooms and a bathroom.

Thankfully there were no broom cupboards – places dark, quiet and out of the way – and I made sure to check for them. I am thankful that Rose and David did not have these kinds of locations to trap me in, but they had worse ways to hurt me – mental and physical ways in which to step inside my psyche and to try to destroy me.

The property itself was set in quite a big garden which was filled with all manner of green vegetables. David was a keen gardener – or, more likely I think, just a tight skinflint who just didn't want to pay for food that he could grow for free. I learned an awful lot about gardening in a short time and it has stayed with me since. David and Rose also grew lots of flowers and trimmed the hedges regularly, causing the place to look lovely, clean and inviting. They would get a whole pig and butcher it into pork joints, pork chops, pig's trotters, and use the head to make brawn and pâté. Things were going pretty well. I got the nickname 'Tiny', as I was apparently skin and bone, and it stayed with me throughout school even though I ended up becoming a big lad for my age.

I worked on the farm when I could. I worked the harvest, stacking bales, and generally enjoyed being outside and with the animals. It was a huge contrast to being an inner city lad, living in the country, and it was fantastic. I devoured the healthy fresh food, breathed in the healthy fresh air and I grew stronger. The taste of freshly grown organic food was something to behold after being used to processed slop. In the homes it was all fish fingers and beans, egg, chips and beans – beans,

beans and beans – various inedible crap and beans… Or just plain beans.

The Burtons had an Irish red setter dog called Sheena, and she was to become my first best friend ever. Dogs just ooze love and affection – if only people were to even take a small leaf out of their book. I talked to Sheena all of the time, we went out for walks whenever possible and we were practically joined at the hip. Sheena sadly died about two years later, which left me heartbroken. But she had raised a litter of nine, of which David and Rose kept the runt – a lovely well-mannered Irish red setter which I named Red. For years, people said that Red wasn't a proper name, and that it was just the colour of the dog – that's why they're called Irish red setters – so I just pointed out that she was named after the American fire fighter Paul Neal 'Red' Adair. Oh, that pissed people off, getting outsmarted by a snotty-nosed kid who should be seen and not heard. I wouldn't let anyone put me down.

Poor Red later got run over and ended up losing her front left leg. She dragged it around for months, and we tried all sorts of exercises that we were advised might get her leg working again, but nothing worked and finally she had to go in for an amputation. The fungus-faced twit that ran her over was my drama teacher from my new school, and boy did he get some stick from me. I was taken out of that class pretty quickly, as well as any other ones they couldn't control me in… I was a teacher's nightmare.

I would rush home from school to see the bullocks, and wake up early at the weekends to feed them. I also helped with the land-drains, which we'd go down and pick up from the merchants, stack on the trailer and drive off in the tractor to lay in the fields. We'd get to the fields – which were mainly around the WW2 Aerodrome in Litchfield, Staffordshire – dig with the 360° JCB track machine and lay down the land-drains. We also had to clear ditches, put pipes in them and backfill them to allow field access. We would also cut wood on a big bansaw which was driven by the power take-off (PTO) shaft on the back of the tractor, and collect grain with the combine harvester. I really loved it on the farm – I loved the work and wished I could just start working there full-time. The Burtons were okay, but I did run away a few times because David and Rose had a 'spare the rod, spoil the child' attitude. But whacking me for something I hadn't done, or for something I didn't understand to be wrong, had no effect – it just made me tougher and resentful. I would just hold things in until I could get my revenge, and there were many, many ways that I could do that. I had practically been to the school of how to get revenge.

All things considered, I was no ordinary kid. I don't think that you can just pick two people out of the air and expect them to be able to look after a foster child effectively. We had different needs, and we'd been through untold traumas. I mostly hid and then got my revenge by running off, throwing things at them and wielding the cane on them if I could get a hold of it.

When I ran off, I didn't go far. The food was good and healthy – and there was plenty of it – and the countryside was magical and ideal for a child, especially one that had rarely seen the outside having been brought up in an inner city environment. So it went on – I'd run off, stay under a car or in a shed overnight, and either go back to the bungalow eventually or get found walking the lanes the following day. Eventually they discovered that if they sent Sheena out she'd find me straight off – so it was really pointless for me to try to escape unless I went miles away. Sheena, who would stand there barking with her cold wet nose and tail wagging ten to the dozen, giving me away. It was all a big game to Sheena, and so I couldn't get angry at her for grassing me up. Running away was really my way of telling them not to mess with me… I wasn't the most eloquent person at the best of times.

But all things considered, I did not under any circumstances want to go back to the children's home. I missed the other kids, but I didn't miss the home or the authoritarian figure, the satanic Mrs Davenport. She was still branded in my mind and she still is to this day.

The Burtons' had a 45-foot-long canal boat moored nearby at Fradley Junction in Staffordshire. So a few times we managed to get away almost as a real family. David was a bit of a drinking man and sometimes he got a little bit violent with Rose, which I noticed more and more, especially within the confines of the canal boat. Dave made excuses for himself as all alcoholics do, he hid his problem, but it came to the surface when he had too much to drink – which was beginning to happen oftener. Rose made excuses for David to try and justify his unjustifiable behaviour. She covered up the bruises and scratches with make-up, but must have not had a mirror because they could be seen quite plainly in the daylight. Of course – she had just slipped on the towpath or the wet floor of the boat, she had fallen and hit her head, and so the charade of cover-up excuses went on. She should have exposed him for what he was there and then: a bully and a control freak. He was not fit to be called a man.

Rose was and still is an attention-seeking control freak herself, with a tongue that could cut steel. Rose drank a lot as well on those breaks, gin and tonic was her tipple, and it would cause her to grow louder and louder. When they got back to the boat, she would say, 'Where's my little bastard?', and I would pretend to be asleep, refusing to stir no matter how much the drunken pair poked and prodded me. I was of course brought up in big dormitories, so playing dead in those situations was second nature to me and an easy act to pull off. The bullying, domestic abuse and wife beating eased on dry land when they got back to the small village, but it still reared its ugly head again when they got back from the pub or from a night out. Thankfully at that stage they only went to the pub on a Saturday night. I would either escape from the bungalow and hide until they passed out, or brave the insults and listen to the fights. Nevertheless, we had good times together in Elmhurst for the short time it lasted, but their demeanour soon changed for the worst under the pressure of their new venture: being the landlord and landlady of the George Inn.

I went to another new school, Nether Stowe secondary in Lichfield – it was a big school of about 2,000 pupils – and I walked across the fields in all types of weather to get there. But my time there was short lived. I was used to moving and getting pushed from pillar to post, but the difference that time was that I didn't want to leave. I had been in Elmhurst for under a year, and I was still just about 13 years old when Rose and David announced that we were going to move to Waterhouses, North Staffordshire as they'd taken on tenancy of a public house. This was my foster parents' long-term dream brought into reality. I didn't get into any trouble at Nether Stowe, except when one lad in the upper years had a go at me one day. I found out his name was Steward Hood, and I figured he must have been the son of the Hoods that had tried to make me write with my right hand. The lad knew my name, and seemed to know me, but I had forgotten him and didn't care who he was, how big he was or anything. By this stage I was a lot stronger – due to working on the farm and eating well – so I gave him a flying head-butt, causing his head to bounce off the steel grate, and kneeled on his back to put an end to his bullying. I didn't even get told off. I think this was because he was an older pupil, and he must have got the piss taken out of him for being bested by a younger kid. The school was good for me, though I still wouldn't play football of course, and I was often sent running around the pitch or sometimes swimming – both of which I enjoyed anyhow.

David and Rose gave their notice in on their day jobs, and before I knew it, we were all packed up and ready to go. It took two trips in a big cattle wagon, which was borrowed from the farmer. In and out of the bungalow like leaf ants, and then in and out of the George Inn with all of our belongings. The two big, deep freezers and the piano were almost deal breakers, but in the end everything succumbed to being moved and the packed bungalow became an empty shell. The George Inn became our new home. I was now 14 years old and had another new school to settle in to.

The school wasn't too bad – I'd been to so many schools at this stage that I'd lost count – but I learned absolutely zero. I was just exhausted all of the time from having to get up early to do chores, and having to stay up late into the night to tend the bar in a smoke-laden, filthy, swearing atmosphere. The children's home in Wolverhampton wasn't good for my mental health, but at least I got schooling and the air wasn't polluted with nicotine, alcohol and foul language. Waterhouses Secondary Modern School was really small in comparison to the big inner city schools I was used to, and there were only about 200 pupils. The teachers got used to my non-conforming attitude and the kids were all woolly-back farmers and country bumpkins, and so they just left me alone. I still didn't play football – I wouldn't play rugby either for a long time for similar reasons – and so I was left to run around the football field or to do cross country. There was a swimming pool there too – happy days.

On more than one occasion I got hauled in to get the cane, slipper or a rap or three on the knuckles with the ruler. It was a breeze and I almost thrived on it. I had been brought up getting whacked, beaten and a whole lot worse from a very young age, and so getting these so-called punishments at school was a chance for me to shine. If I got the cane, I would squeal like a pig even though it didn't hurt a bit; I was playing an emotional game which was well-rehearsed and almost genetically implanted into me on account of a succession of abuse incidents from a succession of children's homes. After my so-called punishment was over, I would take my telling off while crocodile tears still rolled down my cheeks. When their pep talk was over, I would slip them a sly, wry smile or even a full-on blatant, belittling, defying grin. The teachers hated it, as any tormentor would. They would look to the floor, embarrassed at their failure, knowing they could do no more – knowing I knew that they could do no more. There was no way these hicks were getting through to a tough inner city kid that had been through the mill and back. There was no way they would expose themselves to my piss-taking ways again. Because of this, a teacher would rarely haul me in more than once.

About a year into my new school in Waterhouses, it was announced that we would be the second-to-last year left, as the school was going to be changed to a primary school on account of its small size. The remaining pupils were given the option to go to a school in Leek, Staffordshire or to stay put in Waterhouses. Most of the kids went to the school in Leek, which was a far better school, though about nine miles away from Waterhouses. David and Rose did give me the option to go to the school in Leek, but I opted to stay put as I had had my fill of school hopping. Waterhouses School was left with no proper teachers, and the remaining dinosaurs were just ambling on to get their retirement. The maths teacher taught woodwork and metalwork, the English teacher taught English and history, and so on. So even if I did want to learn anything, I couldn't – though I was practically illiterate at that stage anyhow.

I got kicked out of the religious education class, French class and metalwork class – so it was more swimming and cross country for me, which I enjoyed. I was still a nightmare pupil. On occasion I reeled out the fire hose and turned it on full bore to soak classes full of kids, in metalwork I threw engine oil onto the red hot forge, which caused an explosion and backdraught of flames and, more often than not, I would stand on the school roof shouting obscenities at anyone who looked up. They wouldn't have been able to teach me anyhow, let's put it that way. I was bored and the school was way too small for me, but it served its purpose enough to get me to the age of 16 and to take two Certificate of Education examinations – one in woodwork and the other in elementary maths. I failed both miserably. I could spell, but I suppose you would have to be able to write properly for that to matter, and I could add up in my head, no problem at all – writing scores on the darts chalkboard and adding up the prices of drinks and food at the bar taught me that. But in terms of everything else, I was at a total loss.

The George Inn was a huge place, about as big as my old children's home. It had a big bar, a lounge bar, a snug bar – which later became a pool room – and an outdoor bar. Sometimes people would just go to the outdoor bar, ring the bell to get attention and get their demijohns filled up from the tap to take home.

This was before the days of the off-licence, so you'd get people who didn't want to be seen ordering alcohol. But anyhow, everyone knew everyone's business in a small remote village like that one, and it seemed like people went out of their way to find out every last little detail about each other. And if they couldn't find out everything then they would invent things that fitted their narrow perspectives. There was a large club room upstairs, which came alive for birthdays, wedding receptions and meetings. There were a couple of benches in the outdoor bar – they were really for people that were waiting for takeout orders or just wanted to be unnoticed while they had a quick slug.

The George Inn had plenty of regulars, and I remember a Harold and Elsie Fern who used to come in most nights and get three flagons of Woodpecker Cider and six bottles of barley wind. The old couple in their 80s must have been permanently oiled, and both had the constitution of an ox. Occasionally someone would persuade Elsie to come in and play the piano and sing. I don't know where that lovely old lady kept her lungs, but she could really belt 'em out. Everyone enjoyed those moments, but times moved on and things changed. Nevertheless, I thank her for those cherished memories she left behind. Old Harold Fern would order Pigtail tobacco for his pipe, which was a constant companion to his nicotine stained bottom lip and teeth. He occasionally cut a bit of Pigtail tobacco off to chew and spit. It was a lovely rich molasses colour – yuk. Those two old people had such wonderful stories to tell, although I couldn't linger for too long before someone shouted for a refill. Harold and Elsie were always upbeat and they loved life

– so inspirational. Unfortunately, you can't get even one drop of water back that's flown under the bridge. If only it was possible to turn back time a little.

We finally settled in and had all things in place – David even commissioned some elm tables, benches and stools to be made by a local carpenter. The elm was cheap and good timber, due to the fact that a lot of elm trees had succumbed to Dutch elm disease and felling them helped stop the spread of it. David and I took out the two big fireplaces and got a local dry stone-wall builder to build new ones to replace them. The replacement fireplaces were made of local limestone and set in lime mortar. They took on a beige, sandy and grey colour, but the limestone gradually turned darker and the lime mortar eventually turned nicotine brown. The hardest part was trying to source two good flat pieces of limestone for each hearth, and some good weathered timber for the two mantle pieces. With the two fireplaces built in-situ, a lick of paint applied to the lounge ceiling, a new carpet laid in the lounge bar, the licence to sell liquor applied for and received and the nameplate of the new licensees, 'Mr and Mrs David Burton', screwed in over the door, the pub was now open for business. We used some of the old tables and chairs that we'd magpied from the huge club room until our new elm tables, benches and chairs arrived.

We later had to strip the paint off the lounge ceilings, ceiling roses and cornices due to nicotine seeping through. We had to wash all of the nicotine off with sugar soap and a chemical that we sprayed on called Fasolve. When the Fasolve was sprayed on, the nicotine dripped off – it was horrible. Apparently, it was what they used to use on buses. After everything was cleaned down, we went on to re-paint the ceilings, cornices and ceiling roses with gloss. It was a job and a half, and two coats of gloss later it looked really good. If any more nicotine got on the paint, it could just be washed off and removed with copious amounts of sugar soap and warm water. Guess who got that job on their day off? Someone then had the bright idea of painting the ceiling roses and cornices to enable the plaster moulded flowers and thistles to show through at their best. Though, to be fair, the end product really did look good.

A few weeks later, with the fireplaces built and the elm tables beginning to arrive, the carpets could be ordered and laid. A menu was formulated and sent to the printers in Waterhouses – which was run by a nice old boy called George, whose two sons spent more time getting ink on pint pots than on paper. The menus finally came and David and Rose started to serve food. The barroom was left as it was, because David and Rose had plans to knock down the party wall and knock through to the outdoor area, leaving the barroom, outdoor and lounge bars as open plan, separated only by soft barriers. They planned for the change in furniture between areas to keep people in their places, and when they finally got around to doing it, it worked. Work on making the pub open plan started during afternoon closing times, and, after the partition walls were knocked down, we ended up with one big room, only delineated by the linoleum, carpet and tiled flooring. The snug bar, now a pool room, had its own way in and out and its own toilets, so if people wanted to sneak in and out for a quick drink while going unnoticed, they could go there.

The next few months were spent slowly refurbishing and upgrading the now working kitchen. Food continued to be served and it was getting busier and busier. We ordered a second-hand oil fired AGA cooker and moved the freezers – that had originally come from the bungalow at Elmhurst – into the garage. David and Rose ended up buying all of the catering equipment from a company called Michael Baines at grossly discounted prices that poor Michael had agreed to whilst half drunk – he was around so often he almost ended up becoming a permanent feature in the bar. In came a deep fryer for chips, fish and other stuff, and a second fryer was ordered for onion rings and burgers when it was discovered that everything would end up tasting of beef burgers and onion rings without it. Food orders came in thick and fast, leading to continued improvements in the kitchen when the pub was closed between 2pm and 6pm. Well, I say closed, but of course I mean only legally – the George Inn never really closed.

The cellar had to be cleaned out, aired, painted, and all of the old stuff turned out. The place was cavernous and had previously been used as a dumping ground. There were several areas to the cellar, including a boiler room, a coal bunker and a wine and spirits section which was cordoned off with a wooden palisade. There was some stock left over from the previous tenant, but none of it was really much use at all. It was my job to get it all sorted out, and one by one I gradually got each area cleared, cleaned and painted. Once a section was cleared, I'd moved the new stock into the area slowly, piece by piece. It took me about two weeks to get the beer cellar cleaned out and painted... And even when I'd finished that, I still had the small wine cellar and coal house to clean out and paint.

Finally, after about five weeks, I had the cellar sorted out and emptied of the years of accumulated rubbish from previous tenants. Now that it was fully cleaned and painted, it was time to get some stock in from the brewery. The George Inn wasn't a free house, so everything went through the brewery. The dray men came and delivered kegs of beer down the drop. They rolled them down a 45° concrete drop, with a flight of steps up the middle about two feet wide. The drop was overlaid with steel rails, which the barrels and crates slid down with a screech. At the bottom of the drop the barrels hit the concrete block with a padded straw lined cushion, causing them to come to an abrupt stop. You could hear the noise and feel the vibrations throughout the pub. The wooden and plastic crates would be caught and stacked at the bottom of the drop as they came off the steel rails. The soda siphons came in dirty, heavy wooden crates, and seemed to just come endlessly. The corona bottles of orangeade, dandelion and burdock, Coca Cola and R. Whites Lemonade all came in wooden crates as well. It was a happy day when we got kit installed so that the soda water and cola both got fed through the main water supply, as a mix of CO_2 and concentrated syrup. The cordials still continued to come in wooden crates for a while, until eventually they were changed to plastic.

The men mainly had bottles of brown mixed with mild beer, so quite a lot of bottles of brown ale were delivered in plastic crates. They were easy to handle and quite light. There was also quite a lot of bottles of light ale and Pils sold, and these also came in plastic crates. Bitter and mild were the most popular choices at that time, as lager was being introduced quite slowly with there only being choice of Hofmeister or Kronenbourg. Lager was mostly drank with a dash of lime or blackcurrant cordial. There was also Strongbow and Woodpecker Cider, both of which were nearly always drank with a dash of blackcurrant.

The women mainly drank lager and lime and brandy and peppermint cordial, but on Saturday nights they had snowballs, which, at the time, had to be mixed by hand with a fork and glass. Get some Advocaat, lime and lemonade and then whisk like crazy. There was of course also Babycham and Cherry B, which the men had when they were feeling flush or needed their head looking at.

Trade soon built up and David and Rosemary turned the George Inn around from a quiet pub into a really busy one, serving food all day. On Monday it was men's darts night, on Tuesday it was women's darts night, Thursday was country and Western night, Friday was Friday, Saturday was skittles and Sunday was country and Western – AGAIN!! There was also cards, crib, bar skittles, dominoes, darts, pool, fruit machines, Space Invaders and Pac-Man every night. David and Rose were natural hosts, they were natural at being able to put on a façade – like most foster parents – and they were natural at being able to turn on and off the 'on-stage' button. But as chameleon-like as they tried to be, their masks slowly slipped the more alcohol they consumed. The public snipes became public fights and their integrity waned more as their dirty washing got aired in public. But the customers enjoyed their displays of embarrassing antics, and some came to the pub just to witness them. Looking back, there wasn't much other entertainment living in a village in Staffordshire – there were only three TV channels – so I can see why they watched, goaded and stirred up David and Rose, encouraging their live amateur dramatics.

My day started with putting bottles on the empty shelves, and carrying stuff up from the cellar. All of the empties that were put in the bottle bin were dumped outside for me to sort out into an empty crate when I got home from school. I'd dust off the shelves, wiping each bottle and making sure the labels were facing the customers, and then I'd take the empty crate outside to be filled with empties later that day. Next, I would clean out all of the dirty ash trays, and wipe down all of the filthy beer-covered pub tables. My next job was to load up the pub tables with upturned bar stools and chairs. I would then mop the tiled floors in the hallways, the toilets and the back of the bar, hoover the carpets in the lounge bar and make the fires in winter. After all that was done, I'd get washed up and make my way to school, which was only about 500 yards away. So that wasn't too bad. Luckily, the kitchen was always left clean as it was a busy food area with staff that cleaned up after themselves. Otherwise, that would have also been loaded onto my pre-school chores.

Being a young lad, I was keen and eager to please, as I never wanted to set foot back inside the walls of a children's home ever again. They say that work will always come to a willing horse, and I can say first hand that there is no truer statement. I worked from dawn until late in the night, except on school days where I worked before and after school. But I still had to work during my school lunch hour, running home to help serve beef burgers and chip butties to hungry school kids. I also had to bottle up every single day and tend the bar every single night, school or no school. It was relentless.

The club room would spring to life every now and again, for parties, wedding receptions, 18th and 21st Birthdays and surprise parties – not that anyone could keep a secret if they wanted too. But before a party could take place, the whole place had to be subjected to the sugar soap and Fasolve treatment. Although the nicotine wasn't as bad as downstairs in the public bar and lounge bar, it was still pretty dire. The place was more rundown too, as it had been badly neglected. I don't think the heating had been turned on up in there for years. The steel-framed windows with leaded lights were in a right state, which meant another job for me in the spare time that I didn't have. Scrubbing and scraping off the rust, I slowly talked each steel window frame into turning. Then, once stripped back and painted, each small rectangular window had to be cleaned. There seemed to be hundreds of them – there were four windows that were five feet high and about seven feet wide, and three smaller windows of the same height that were only four feet wide. It took weeks on end until they were finally completed and painted from top to bottom.

After I was done, Rose and David said, 'Oh, leave serving behind the bar tonight, it will allow you to catch up with finishing the club room – we know you want to get it done.' They said it as if they were doing me a big favour. I was exhausted, and for good measure I went downstairs for a rest – only I had to walk through the bar to get to my bed in the private accommodation end of the building. And then it was, 'Oh love, just pull a couple of pints for these lads while I go into the kitchen.' So there they sat in the bar, getting drunk, never going near the bloody kitchen. And towards the end of the evening it was, 'Oi, you little bastard get over here and do this or that', or, 'Stop loitering and pull these pints.'

When there was a party or something I had to get the club room ready, which meant cleaning it and getting the bar set up. Crates of bottles had to be hauled up from the cellar, and then dusted and cleaned so that the customers could see the labels. The beer barrels had to be brought up the day before to allow the beer to settle and to get all of the beer coolers set up and working. Then of course, post-party, the place had to be cleaned from top to bottom. Empty bottles were taken outside and put into the correct crates for return, and unsold stock was hauled back down into the cellar.

The club room later became a dormitory for construction workers, who were working on a large project at the local Blue Circle Cement Works. There wasn't much else in the way of cheap accommodation in the area at that time, so amongst all the other things I got more work tagged onto my load. I made a bit of money on the side running errands – fetching sandwiches and beer from downstairs in the bar. The workers were mainly Irish and from Birmingham – the sort of people I worked with years later when I got a job in construction myself in Birmingham, where I now live.

David and Rose, in general, rarely cooked me a meal or washed my clothes. I did it all myself. But I was 14, and so it was no hardship. There were school dinners that consisted of the same crappy cheap food I had been used to in care, and so I raided the fridge in the kitchen when I got up and David and Rose were still in bed, stinking and farting. I'd go to school and come back during the lunch hour to work in the kitchen, as the school kids swamped the place for chip butties and burgers during that time. When school finally ended, I would get the chance to either swim or do some running for an hour to clear my head, but when I got back 'home', I would end up working behind the bar until late in the night. I'd also try to get ahead of putting up the bottles and cleaning to take the weight off myself for the next day. I would try to usher the 'stay back crew' out of the lounge bar, so that I could empty the ashtrays, wipe the tables and upturn some stools onto the big, rustic elm tables.

The pool room was only small, so I sometimes cleaned it first, sweeping it, mopping it and taking the empty and half-full glasses off the shelves that surrounded the room. There were only four small tables in there, so it was an easy job to tick off my list. I dreaded the weekends because there was no school, and I'd end up peeling at least fifty kilos of potatoes, most of which I had to cut into chips by hand. After that would be the vegetables. I hated doing Brussels sprouts, as each had to have a cross cut into the bottom stalk, to enable ease of cooking, without the head being spoilt. My hands were wet all of the time, and it was often freezing cold on the Staffordshire moorlands. The garage I did most of this work in was oppressive, with draughts blowing in from all angles. I tried to stop these by wedging cloth underneath, on top of and to the sides of the big wooden doors, but it was really no use. Even in the summer, it was cold, draughty and wet in there.

I ended up collapsing once and had to be taken to the hospital, where I was laid up for six weeks and diagnosed with rheumatic fever. The local doctor also thought he heard a murmur whilst using his stethoscope, which I'm convinced was bronchitis or wheezing brought on by the smoke-filled bar rooms. The stumped, bemused country doctor couldn't bring himself to accept that I was being used as a slave – especially when his surgery was right next door to the garage where I was entombed for most of the time. He couldn't allow himself to see what was before his eyes. If he had just put two and two together, he would have seen that I was a victim of slavery, child abuse and child neglect. It was quite visible that I was walking around like a wretch, and there was no secret in the fact that I tended the bar practically all of the time. It was a small village, and they poked their noses into every little bit of gossip they could find, so they must have known about me. Fine, upstanding, decent people? More like a bunch of hypocritical bastards.

On reaching North Staffordshire Hospital in Stoke-on-Trent – about 18 miles away from Waterhouses – they examined me but still couldn't find any anomalies. I was taken in for an electrocardiogram, or ECG, but they still could not find any anomalies with my heart. I was put in an isolation ward and prescribed to take amoxicillin until I was 40 years old, just in case I got an infection that could kill me. But I didn't take the pills. The main thing I could never understand was why the pub-using punters didn't report this. I knew no different; I was conditioned into a slave lifestyle from an early age – a product of the so-called care system.

I was soon back to cleaning, peeling vegetables and tending the smoke-filled bar rooms, but never fell ill or collapsed again. Obviously, David and Rose didn't learn anything – they really didn't care at all if I lived or died as long as I got my daily chores done. They must have had a shock when I was put in hospital for those six weeks, but it made no difference to them whatsoever. Now that is callous intent...

Was there a duty of care owed? Was the duty of care broken? Were wrongs committed as a result? The answer is a clear yes to all three of those questions – countless wrongs were committed – which are the basis for every criminal claim in the UK even today still.

One day I found a letter from my mother with a picture of my father enclosed – I will never forget that photo. I read the last page of the letter, and it said,

'I have enclosed a picture of your dad Horace, please return it to me as it's the only one I have. I had it in my purse when they took me away from you.

I have always loved you and I will love you until the day I die.

Your loving mum.'

I heard someone coming and so, not wanting to arouse suspicion, put the letter back where I had found it, went about my chores and left for school. The next morning, I looked where I'd put it, but it was gone. And so I never did get a chance to return the picture of my father to my mother – I never even saw the return address on the letter. I agonised for years about what my mother must have thought of me for this. I knew it was my foster parents that had stolen it from me, and they had no doubt burnt it. Even they must have felt guilty and agonised over letting me have the picture of my father. But at least I got to see a glimpse of him. I won't forget his face and I thank my mother for that, even though it must have caused her great pain. Rose and David Burton must have thought that they were controlling me with their actions, but I wasn't bothered about them in any way – they were just something stuck to the bottom of my shoe. I only stayed with them because I didn't want to go back into care.

Another strange thing occurred to me at that moment: I had regularly been given letters to put into the postbox on my way too school with the name crossed out on the envelope, and, above the address for the George Inn, 'Not at this address – return to sender'. Those sick, perverse bastards had made me put letters intended for me, from my birth mother, into the letterbox. I cannot understand what sort of kick they got from it – so bloody insulting it makes me sick. I later found out that my mother had been writing to me regularly for years, and it had all just been kept from me. I never knew.

The letter from my mother raised some serious questions in my mind, and brought back some long absent memories from before I was taken away from my family by the state. Is she my real mother? Is she still alive? Where does she live? Have I got brothers and sisters? Have I got any aunties and uncles – cousins? Is the man in that photograph my real father? Where is my father? Is he still alive? Why don't my parents come and get me? And, mostly, why does the man in the photograph have the same face as the man in my nightmares?

The questions kept getting generated, one after another. I then thought about different scenarios of what would eventually happen to me. What was going to become of me? Could I carry on working like this? Would I just collapse and die one day?

Eventually I came to the conclusion that if I did have a family, and they left me in those homes to fend for myself, then I really didn't want to know them. So why torture myself about it all? I thought, 'I need to survive right now, right here and on my own.' I knew that my torment would soon be over as I was approaching 16, and that when I was 18 I would be out of the hands of social services... Bloody roll on.

One evening my foster parents broached the subject of adoption too me. I was a bit taken aback and suspicious. Making some lame excuse, I carried on with my work and later said I'd think about it and let them know as soon as I'd made a decision. I wondered why they were being so unusually friendly and not shouting at their little bastard to do this and that for them. They also knew that I was a tricky person to deal with, and that I would sniff out any crafty attempts at entrapment in an instant. I wasn't bright academically, my schooling record was poor, but I knew people, I knew deceit and I knew life. Emotionally, I'd already lived through five or more lifetimes. I had a hair trigger temper at the time and so they wouldn't push me too much. I didn't accept or decline, but said I would think about their proposal.

With my mind doing summersaults, and my emotions running riot, I weighed up the options before me. Did I want to get adopted? I wasn't sure... Did I want to return to the home with Mrs Davenport? Definitely not. Would things change when I got adopted? Probably not, but I could make demands.

By getting adopted, would it mean I could run away without those council bastards being able to do anything? Was this initiated by the social services or David and Rose? You have me cornered, don't ya? You know you can hold my balls, but you ain't twistin' 'em?

The internal debate went on. I was confused, but I knew I didn't want to go back to the home, so I spoke to David and Rose and agreed to be adopted.

A week later two men walked into the George Inn. Even though I'd never seen those men before – and like coppers they try to be inconspicuous – they were instantly recognisable as social workers, sticking out like a zit on a conk. The pair of incognito dummies took a seat, ordered some drinks and gawkily looked around, weighing the place up. They did everything except cut holes in their newspapers and look through them. They were probably asking themselves whether it was a suitable environment for a child to be brought up in. Would they recognise one if they saw it, I pondered.

They were so dumb that they didn't really see me observing them, not even asking themselves what a 15-year-old kid was doing in a public bar or why the customers were shouting, 'Come on Tiny, you gonna pull us a couple of pints or what?' The dummies were still weighing the place up. Well, I think they probably weren't actually, they would have to consult their generic forms first, just to see if there was a yes or no box they could tick that reflected the situation. If they had been doing their blooming job properly in the first place, they would have spot-checked and seen me peeling spuds in squalid conditions, tending a smoke-filled bar late into the night, and mopping and bottling up early in the morning before school. But I suppose that was out of their 9am to 5pm remit. They should have first gone to the local school to interview me with the teachers present, though it's a bloody good job that they didn't because I would have been hauled back into care straight off, no question.

The two social workers finally introduced themselves to a shocked and surprised Dave and Rose, who should have both won first-rate Oscars for their performances. The pair of dummies asked for a meeting with them first and David and Rose informed them that the pub was closed from 2:30pm to 5pm, and asked if they would like something to eat while they waited. So it was agreed and lunch was served to the two dummies. After they had eaten their lunches, they went off for their meeting. Dave and Rose already had their on-stage switches on and were laughing and joking with their hosts. If the dummies had looked hard enough they would have seen the bruises on Rose's eye and forehead. Though even if they had seen them, they would have been explained away as a fall anyway – there were numerous scenarios waiting to spring out in defence of David the wife-beating bully, because, of course, he was an upstanding member of the community.

After they'd finished, it was my turn to get a question and answer session from the two social workers. I was well-accustomed to their daft, generic questions at that stage. And so they went on with their perverse, demeaning, assuming, accusatory questions, all with no discussion and no room for manoeuvring. 'Yes or no only, Keith – yes or no…' I was daft, but I wasn't deaf.

Do they touch you? Do they ask you to touch them? Do you have feelings for them? Do they bathe you? Do they dress you? Do they hit you?

And so the perverse, emotionless, generic questions went on. No real conversation, no treating me as an adult and no treating me as a human full stop. I was a statistic, to be spied on and treated like a lab rat – existing for experimental purposes only.

I gave them the answers they wanted to their yes/no questions. The straight-faced, dower, emotionless freaks couldn't recognise or cope with the truth, and besides, they had probably ticked all of the boxes and filled the form in while they were munching on their free ploughman's lunch earlier. All I had to do to keep me from going back to the home was to go along with their charade, and I'd soon be 18 years old so they could swing for all I cared. The bastards would have locked me up if I'd done a runner, which is a bit ironic really – they overlook the trauma and bad treatment you're going through, but if you run off they come down on you like a ton of bricks. They were always watching – they were always there in the background – and they'd given my mother my address for sure. Where else could she have got it?

The bastards just wouldn't let me go, and they were not content until they had interfered with me in every way possible. They were relentless.

Then came the million-dollar suggestion from the two social workers. They said, 'Right, Keith, sign the form at the bottom and we'll deal with the rest on your behalf. We will sort out the name change from Lawton to Burton, and then you will be legally adopted into your new loving family.'

In an instant my back straightened, my eyes glared, and I said, 'Name change? Are you mental? I'm not changing my name for you or anyone else.'

They tried to justify the name change by telling me that it was all just part of the process. 'Be a good boy now and sign the form,' they retorted in a demeaning, 'grow up, you silly little child' attitude. Of course, none of that good cop, bad cop routine worked with me. They were probably ex-squaddies, retiring police or something – you know the type, you can tell by their attitude, and their stumbling, clumsy method of trying to do a job that they couldn't do in a month of Sundays. They just didn't have the skills, training or aptitude for it – they couldn't handle it at all in any way shape or form – and now, on the back foot, they were out of their depth and struggling to keep control of the situation. They tried every angle to get me on side, to manipulate me, but I was well-versed in dealing with pricks like them. I had put up with bullshit like theirs all my life.

So the ping-pong game went on, back and forth, with me leading them up the garden path and into the stinging nettles patch. But eventually the game of cat and mouse wore off, and I wasn't going to play anymore. I started banging my spoon in my bowl, and the toys were coming out of the pram one by one. So characteristically, I got mad, and they got defensive, shooting me that look – that look of bemusement and amazement all people wear when they are on the losing side of an argument. The look that says, 'I can't believe you.' It says, 'Are you stupid or something? This is the deal of a lifetime, and I believe wholeheartedly that I am right and you are wrong. What a shock – did that really happen? I didn't mean it that way. I really didn't mean to offend you, just sign here and we will be on our way.'

I had news for them – their bullying, demeaning tone wasn't about to best me in any way and it had gained no mileage or momentum with me whatsoever. I was bloody right and they knew it, so I got mad and my blood rose. I tried to control myself, but eventually the pot boiled over and I gave them both barrels as they left the room. I signed nothing, and I kept my name as Lawton because I was, and still am, me. My DNA isn't part of any other line, and never will be – that is a fact that no one can change. The dismayed, beaten social workers eventually left after being met with eye rolling. Thanks to David and Rose's performances, I didn't see them or any other of those dummies again. Now all I had to do was keep up with my workload until I was 18 years old and free from the care of social services – I knew that they were still there in the background, and my file proved it.

Instead of the social workers presenting their perverse questions to you as though somehow 'you' are the problem, perhaps the questions asked should be focused on your surroundings, such as your foster parents and the school you go to. For example:

Do these people exploit you for financial gain?
Do these people deny you a proper education?
Do these people hit each other?
Can you read this passage out loud? (With this question they should compare your reading age with your actual age.)
Can you transcribe this short passage?
Can you do the following maths test?

And each of these questions on the form should be accompanied by a comments section – the questioner should be able to put down more than just a 'yes' or 'no'. They should also make note of things such as the child's cleanliness and weight…

Questions like these would have indisputably shown abuse, and indisputably highlighted the lack of care shown to me. And if not, they would have enabled the social workers to raise concerns and investigate further. If they had tried talking to me, instead of at me, then perhaps I would have responded better. They talked accusatorily, as if I were a hardened criminal, and they were ready to pounce at any moment – to taser me and zip tie my hands and feet. No, I wasn't going to tell them anything. No other orphan that had been through the same stuff would. That is the point, that's why they get away with their aloofness and lack of care, because they know you are lying. The next time they get more standoffish and distance themselves from you even more – we can see the barriers even if they can't, and no amount of training or experience will ever allow them to see them. Not unless they stop treating us like imbecilic nothings, and not unless they treat us with the respect that all kids deserve.

Perhaps arranging an interview with you at the local school would shed more light on what the social workers needed to know? I, like most, just lied anyhow to keep myself from going back to Mrs Davenport – anyone else would have done the same. You cannot win against those people, with their attitudes towards us – we're just pesky peasants locked outside the castle walls. 'How dare they, how impertinent of them – we'll show them how to step in line. Tally ho.'

David and Rose continued to fight like cat and dog, much to the punters' delight and much to my own detriment. There was another pub about a mile away called Ye Olde Crown, and the landlord and landlady, Dennis and Prudence, also displayed their fights publicly like David and Rose. I'd witnessed them myself. The punters started to come to the George Inn from the Olde Crown when Dennis and Pru were too sober to be arguing. They'd try to play Dennis and Pru off against each other to get them falling out for entertainment value. When that failed they would come to the George to try the same routine on an unsuspecting Dave and Rose. Everyone could see it but themselves. They were so wrapped up in their own little world that they had become oblivious to anything or anyone else. Eventually Rose ended up getting attention from one of the construction workers' electrical contractor bosses, and they ended up eloping together, later getting married. So, in effect, my so-called carefully vetted foster parents got divorced, leaving me once again orphaned. They robbed me of my youth and even my schooling. The George Inn went downhill, fuelled by my foster father's continued alcoholism and violence.

David was a very clever individual, despite his former work as a farm labourer and current job as the landlord of the pub. But alcohol didn't suit him one little bit – he'd become detached from himself. The George Inn strangled David and Rose – the long hours, the seven days a week and the 365 days a year. They did have some really good staff, but they tried so hard to do all of the work themselves and ended up taking their eyes off the ball. The idea of standing at the end of the bar with a tie on, chatting to varied customers, was soon brought into reality. In actual fact it was glorified plate spinning – whilst playing keep-me-up – running around serving sometimes awkward cantankerous people and dashing into the kitchen to fulfil food orders, whilst customers banged their glasses on the bar and shouted for service. You could almost sense them waiting for a lone working Dave or Rose to go to the kitchen before swallowing the last dregs of their pint and shouting for more. Of course they did it on purpose, and that amongst other things took its toll on Dave and Rose – it would be their downfall. They were on the face of it quite nice people, but totally incompatible as a couple. Chalk and cheese. I think I must have Stockholm syndrome.

With Rose gone, David tried to keep the George Inn afloat on his own, but he just got worse and really fell off the wagon. The staff got a higher workload, and one by one the part-time workers left. Each that left put a bigger burden on the remaining staff, each that left put more pressure on David and each that left put more work my way. I was enduring Spring tides of work on a daily basis. Eventually David had no staff left at all and the customers kept coming. People would call in due to the George's good reputation, and sometimes they'd turn on their heels, sometimes they'd stay and sometimes they would get up from their table and leave after waiting too long to be served food or even met at all. It all became too much. The worsening of his drinking, the falling standards of cleanliness, the stained shirt, the unshaven face and David's demeanour all contributed to the George Inn's downfall – and quite rightly too.

One day he got his hand around my throat, pinned me against the wall and said, 'I can live without you, but you can't live without me.' He could not have predicted my response: I looked into his eyes with defiance in mine. He said, 'You're not afraid of me, are you?' I didn't reply, and he let me go, walking away distraught, with his head bowed. He learned more about me in those couple of seconds than he had in all of the time I'd been fostered out to him. He also learned more about himself in those few seconds than he had in a lifetime. He'd been beating on his wife Rose throughout their marriage, but when confronted with a grown man that was willing to fight back, the gutless coward couldn't do it. I never saw David again.

The next day, very early in the morning, I got up and left home. I had a little bit of money saved, made up of that given to me by the construction workers for running errands and tips from waiting tables for food customers. The only other thing I had were the clothes on my back and a bag with bread and meat in it. I was stood at the side of the road with my thumb out, waiting for a lift out of Waterhouses and for a chance to start my new life – wherever it might be. I had little confidence and little education, but I was determined to start over somewhere new – anywhere new.

I met Burt the postman as he rode past on his bicycle. He had always been a friendly man – he knew everyone on account of his job – and he used to go into the George Inn in the afternoon between 1pm and 2:30pm. He'd have a cheese sandwich, a plate of chips and a half pint of bitter, and just talk the head off anyone that would listen. He probably went home to bed afterwards, ready for his early start the next day. Burt knew I was leaving home. He'd also witnessed my treatment, and he told me that others had also spoken to him showing concern. I asked him why someone hadn't blown the whistle on David and Rose, but I got no real answer. I wasn't skilled at asking questions, with my lack of confidence being the result of so-called adults controlling me all of my life, and I'd never really spoken to anyone in such a capacity before. I asked people what they wanted to drink or eat, but that was the height of my conversational skills. I pressed Burt for answers, but he simply hung his head down.

Burt asked me if I was still writing to my mum, and I said I'd never written to her as I had no idea where she was. I was then reminded of what I'd discovered before, that David and Rose had been hiding her letters from me.

Burt said, 'As the postman I am not supposed to tell you this, but she's been sending letters addressed to you for many years.' I was so mixed up by this stage, and did not know what was true or false. Burt went on to say that my mother had also been sending me postcards from some seaside place – addressed to me with 'your loving mum' at the end. So, as the handwriting was the same as that on the envelopes, he guessed that it had been my mother who had been writing to me over the years.

I was to later find out that my mother had been moved to a care home in Clacton-on-Sea, Essex. So, when I did eventually find out, it confirmed that Burt had been right all along. I thanked Burt, stuck my thumb out and hitched a ride out of Waterhouses. I couldn't help but think of the letter I'd gotten a glimpse of with my father's picture inside, I couldn't shake off the nightmares of the man with my father's face, holding his hands out and screaming in pain, I couldn't stop the tears and I couldn't understand the pain. I was boiling inside, knowing that David and Rose had, unbeknownst to me, made me post my own mother's mail in the postbox whilst on my way to school, marked: 'Not at this address – return to sender'. However, it was comforting to know that some people were human and did care. The lesson it taught me was to never turn the other cheek, to always be alert of similar things happening to others and to tell people and confront people.

Torquay

My lift took me to Leek, a small market town in North Staffordshire. I then asked locally if someone could point me towards the motorway, got to the A53 and thumbed a lift to Stoke-on-Trent. From there I got onto the M6 and headed south. I ended up in Torquay of all places, and it was unlike anywhere I'd ever seen – it was incredible to my eyes. I got a bus to the town centre, and then I took a short walk to the seafront. It was all so clean, bright and green – I couldn't believe my eyes. I had never seen anywhere that was so pristine and pretty. There were palm trees, and flowers seemed to be planted everywhere – down low in immaculately manicured flower beds, up high in the hanging baskets that were on every lamppost and up even higher on the balconies and the window boxes of hotels, bars and guest houses. There were little walks through overhanging vegetation. There were steep steps up that led to different places, and houses seemed to be perched all over the hills. It was a real feast for the eyes and the imagination, and food for the soul.

I just wanted to go down to the seafront and look. Nothing else, just sit and look. The next few hours were spent partaking in my favourite pastime – still to this day: people watching. Holiday makers were out swimming, boating, water-skiing, playing and sunbathing, yet another feast for the eyes; it was incredible to me. Now there were no more chores, no bartending late into the night and no more early mornings – I was free from the yolk. It was, in fact, quite surreal; almost as though it was all in my head. After years of tyranny in one form or another, I could finally just sit and contemplate on my next move. I became a tree at every opportunity, and my own genetic self slowly came filtering through as I mapped out my future path using my limited perspective on life. As the long day drew on – I had left Waterhouses in the early morning of that day and arrived in Torquay at about 2pm – I was getting beat. Romantic ideas of sleeping on the beach overnight didn't seem very appealing in reality.

I had to find somewhere to stay, as I was really tired after my whole day of hitchhiking and travelling. Having eaten all of my bread and meat whilst waiting on the roadside for different people to pick me up, I wasn't at all hungry. I had never seen so many hotels, they seemed to be everywhere, and I knew the ones on the seafront would be the most expensive, so I walked a little way inland, up Union Street and through the town centre. Finally, I got into Ellacombe, where I found a small bed & breakfast on St. Marychurch Road with the sign 'vacancy' in the window. Every other place seemed to be full up, and I was dead on my feet. I walked up the short concrete path, lined with seashells imbedded into mortar, and rang for attention. The elderly landlady came and looked at me with suspicion as I asked for a room. I didn't look like a holiday maker, and I had no case or anything else.

'Yes, I do have a vacancy,' she said, 'but not just for one night. How long were you thinking of staying for?' I told her I wanted somewhere for at least two weeks, and that I was down in Torquay looking for work. I also added that I had money to pay upfront if she wanted it. The landlady could see I was skint, and I probably looked pale and gaunt from being held as a virtual prisoner cum slave in the George Inn. Her terms seemed favourable to me, although I really didn't have a clue as to how much it was normal to pay for a room in a B&B. I booked in for seven nights at £10 a night. I slept straight after I got into my room, only waking up when I got a knock on the door asking if I wanted full English or continental. I didn't have a clue what the lady was on about, so I shouted my reply, 'Full English, please.' I rushed to get dressed and when I got downstairs I ate everything in sight. I asked for more toast, and the landlady must have thought that I was going to eat the plates next and then the tablecloth... She'd make no profit with me eating everything in sight.

After finishing, I got up and went straight down to the seafront again. I sat and people watched for what seemed like hours on end. Eventually I walked down to the harbour to marvel at the boats. It was an incredible sight to my eyes, to see so many different types of yachts, the bells at the top of their masts making cowbell noises in harmony. There were so many people wandering around, waiting for boat trips and just looking like me. I walked as far around the harbour as I could, only stopping to take in different aspects on my way around. One thing I really remember was the light itself, it seemed to be so much brighter and bluer than it ever was in Waterhouses. The light shining off the sea itself was mesmerising – silver, gold, every shade of blue and the odd flash of blinding white light, making my eyes squint to narrow slits. The smell of the sea air comforts you like nothing else, and the breeze just seems to send your troubles aloft, cleansing your thoughts and unburdening your mind. After a full day of exploring my surroundings, doing a bit of sight-seeing and a lot of walking, I knew Torquay was the place I wanted to be. *This is where I'll be happy and make my home, whatever it takes.*

After getting back to the bed & breakfast guest house and lying in my bed – looking out of the skylight of the attic room – I knew I had to face reality and find work. I had to get an income. I really didn't know what to do, but I did know how to peel potatoes, prepare vegetables and wash dishes, so I asked at various hotels for work. I eventually got a job washing dishes and got paid £10 a day, enough to pay for my attic room, and I could eat all I liked too. I worked seven days a week for two hours between 8am and 10am for breakfast, and then 6pm and 8pm for the evening meal. Then, with my belly filled, I would go home. I had enough money for the bed &

breakfast for about three more weeks, so I paid the landlady up front, saved all of my wages and then got a small bedsitting room on Brunswick Terrace, near to my new place of work. I stayed there for quite a long time, as it was also only a stone's throw away from the Torbay Tech College.

The hotel I worked at for the longest was the Beachmore Hotel, just behind the Police Station and just off South Street opposite the Lansdowne Hotel. The Beachmore was run by Norman and Sue, who were from Huddersfield, and between the two of them, they could have you in stitches with laughter all day. The people at the Lansdowne were Ray and June, and they were from the West Midlands – Wolverhampton, I think. My, they were so comical too. Ray was so funny, and I spent many an hour there with them. I did washing up there also. Ray and June had two kids, Rob and Sally, and they were brilliant with me and also blessed with good humour. It was a breath of fresh air to me, to find that these people could be so nice and treat me like a human being. I had no faith in adults whatsoever – so many of them had done me wrong in one way or another, and treated me with suspicion, with contempt and/or like a child. Most adults I'd met previously I'd seen in disdain, and not the other way around. They were cowards for not speaking up about my treatment at the hands of others. They didn't speak up about things because they were afraid of losing their jobs, being tarred with the same brush and most of all they were just afraid of the consequences.

Washing dishes was a doddle. There was no draughty, cold, wet garage to endure, there was no constant vegetable peeling to do, and all in all it was an ideal job for a young person. Although if my hands come in to contact with lemon washing up liquid now, they come out in a rash – sensitising dermatitis, I think they call it – a great excuse for dodging the dishes in later life. Breakfast was served between 8am and 10am and dinner was served between 5pm and 7pm, so the best hours for me to do the washing up were 8am until 10:30am and 5pm until 7:30pm. This left my day free from 10:30am until 5pm. Brilliant. All of my spare time was spent exploring my new surroundings, and I went further afield each day, taking different routes on the local bus service. I even went to the beach to sunbathe (taking into account the limited amount of days the British summer would allow for it.) So basically, I had time on my hands and all I could eat after however many guests either didn't get up for breakfast or make it for the evening meal. The less the merrier – more for my belly.

Also, for extra cash, there were things to do at the seafront, such as handing out flyers and leaflets. I would also tell younger holiday makers what the best nightclubs and boat trips were, and give them local knowledge of what deals different pubs had on food and drink. At night I worked in different night clubs collecting and washing glasses. Sometimes I was made to work on the door, but I shirked that as much as I could to get in and mingle with the crowd of revellers glass collecting, having a boogie and getting free drinks. All in all, with all of my mini-part-time jobs, I earned a good living. There was no paying for food, drink was in the main free an entry to nightclubs was free. As I knew most of the door people and bar staff, I was able to get in anywhere on my nights off without charge, and more often than not the beer wouldn't cost me a thing either.

During the winter, I'd get work at various hotels, decorating, cleaning and laying patios. Digging for a swimming pool at the Beachmore Hotel was a laugh – my god, none of us had a clue – but the job got done and the pool liner fitted like a glove over the blockwork. And just as we were laying down the last slabs and blocks, the first guests arrived for the summer. Phew, close call. It was bloomin' hard work for little reward, but hearing the humour of Norman and Sue was worth far more than any amount of money. I learned to do a lot of these sorts of jobs from others, and I found I loved building work. And as much as I loved Norman and Sue, and Ray and June from across the road at the Lansdowne, I knew I couldn't work for them forever and had to get a proper job.

My education had been inconsistent on account of being moved from pillar to post frequently. Because I was brought up in so many different care homes, I had no qualifications – not good at all. I had been to multiple schools as a child and never learned anything much as all of the schools had been incompatible, and the two to three week stints with various different foster parents just messed up my learning even more. When I slaved in the George Inn for David and Rose I never learned anything either, because I was up really early working before school and up most of the evening breathing in cigarette smoke whilst working behind the bar – I was too young to be doing that. So I had to try to educate myself the best way I could; I really wanted to learn. I do remember at one point that – bear in mind how messed up in the head I was – I thought it would be a good idea to smash a window in the high street so I'd get locked up, in order to get an education in prison. It probably wasn't a bad idea, though thankfully I didn't go down that route even though most in my situation, with my history, would.

Eventually I broached the subject to Norman and Sue. This was a big step for me, but I really needed help and advice. I'd never trusted any adults with anything before, let alone let them know my feelings. True to form, they were both so kind and considerate that I was bowled over. I cried and made myself look like a right plank, but they understood my anguish – those wise people that I loved with all my heart. Sue went and got me some information from the Torbay College of Arts and Technology, and I went there with her the next day to see someone on reception. Sue could talk them through my lack of education, and find out what the receptionist thought best suited my needs. On the advice of the receptionist, I went for an interview with a tutor, who assessed me further. At first they were not at all interested, but I persisted and ended up taking night classes for English and basic elementary maths. It took me three attempts to get a grade C in English, and I didn't pass maths at all.

With my washing up job and my new job as a glass collector at Claire's Nightclub, I was earning quite a bit and had free time during the day. I went to the dole place and I managed to get housing benefits for my small room/bedsit – £40 per week and some social security money. With my spare time, I went to the Torbay Technical College and enrolled in an O-level maths course and an O-level human biology course, both of which I passed with a grade 'B'. I wasn't thick after all, and I wanted to learn lots more if I could.

When I got my results I asked if I could go on and do A-levels and the principal said that it would be no problem. But because I was too honest and said I was collecting social security, they said I couldn't attend over 22 hours of college per week unless I signed off from it. So this left me unable to start the course. They said I could apply for a grant, and I tried that, but it was the same old story: no fixed abode and no family history. Perhaps smashing a window on the high street might not have been a bad idea after all. Aftercare my eye – they let you down, stamp on you, let you down and stamp on you some more. I was trying so hard to get on, trying to pull myself up by my own bootlaces, trying so hard with no family, but would the state help? Not bloody likely. I knew the only way forward was to find other work, something more consistent that was somewhere I could learn and grow, and that paid a good wage. I loved being outdoors and walked endlessly in my spare time – also running and swimming when I could – and so I knew I needed an outdoor job. I knew I needed to do a manual job to suppress my endless energy, and it had to be something worthwhile so I could grow.

Walking along the seafront one weekday afternoon, I saw some workmen putting up hoarding fencing. I asked one lad who they worked for because I was looking for work. The workmen pointed me in the direction of a group of wooden huts – they were construction site offices, but I didn't know that at the time. I met with the foreman and he told me to come back on Monday at 7am with a pair of steel toe cap boots and a hard hat. The next day I went to the Beachmore and told Norman and Sue my news. They were so kind and seemed happy for me, and they told me that if I didn't like the job after a couple of weeks that they would find some work for me to do at the Beachmore. I really needed to know where I could buy a pair of steel toe cap boots and a hard hat, so Norman drove me down to the army and navy store to sort me out with the stuff I needed. I walked out of the store with a German parker coat, a pair of high laced boots and an uncomfortable white plastic hard hat.

Monday morning came, I was introduced to the ganger man and off I went. No waiting around for inductions and looking for competence cards those days, it was just up, out and straight to work. The building I worked on for the next two years was the new Torbay Conference Centre, which was for the construction firm Christiani & Nielsen. It was to be a big, imposing, concrete-framed building. But first things first, I helped the gang that was erecting the perimeter hoarding fencing. The site itself was starting to be stripped of grass and vegetation, with tipper wagons coming and going, taking full loads away and returning empty, ready for another load to go.

The reduced dig continued until there was a big hole in the ground – the footprint of the new building. They then introduced a compacted layer of stone over a section of the construction site, as it had to be piled due to unforeseen ground conditions. The Torbay Conference Centre was to be founded on these piles that were essentially reinforced concrete columns with diameters of about 750mm, drilled down and toed in on the bedrock to give support to the building. The existing ground was like a stained red limestone, but it was broken up like loose shale and was full of voids due to the artesian springs that peppered the site. When one section was complete, the process was repeated on other sections until everywhere on-site that was part of the footprint of the Torbay Conference Centre was piled. This piling was all completed by a company called Cementation. There seemed to be red- coloured muck, mud, loose rocks and slurry all over the site, and, quite frankly it was good when they had finished and left... And I say that in the nicest way possible.

The reduced dig to the sub-formation of the building began with us digging around the concrete pilings to expose the top 1.5 metres or so that needed to be cut off and removed from the site. We cut around the concrete piles at what they call 'cut off' level, and then we broke them down with jackhammers. It was really hard work, but I loved it – I was made for it really. There were no so-called 'trigger times' as they have today, where you are only allowed so long on the jackhammer before they take you off – or the machine cuts off automatically when it's time to rest. Once the piles were cut off, all of the ground was levelled off and the access material was removed. After a section was completed, it would receive a layer of concrete blinding.

We had to keep the area dry as best we could, but it was difficult to say the least because the site was littered with artesian springs. Water seemed to bubble up all over the site. Because the construction site was only 500 metres away from the seafront, it was in a low spot and the water was continually accumulating from the surrounding hills. The slightest drop of rain would leave the site submerged for about two hours, after the water had filtered down from the surrounding hills. The whole site had to be lined with a bitumen-based product layer to prevent the water from coming into what was to be the new building. The product used was Bituthene. We primed the area with bitumen primer paint, and then we overlaid the area with Bituthene, peeling off the paper as we went, so eventually whole sections were covered in the stuff. We avoided walking on it with our boots on for fear of the clerk of works spotting a hole in the system, and if we did then there would more often than not be a puddle of water on top of the hole to give the game away.

With the Bituthene layer laid down, the area was overlaid with a protective layer of Servipak – a bitumen felt-like sheet. The Servipack was then overlaid with another layer of concrete blinding to enable the steel reinforcing to be laid on top. The whole of the Torbay Conference Centre building was effectively encased in a bitumen plastic bag to keep it dry – this is called tanking. When the base was completed, the perimeter retaining walls of the building were built for the underground car park. All of the retaining walls were covered in bitumen paint, then we applied more Bituthene, overlaid it with Servipak and backfilled behind the retaining walls to get out of the ground. With the building at last out of the water, the rest of it could be built with ease.

As work progressed over the two year build process, I found myself laying the drainage, helping lay concrete – with different finishes – helping the steel-fixers who made cages out of rebar and, of course, my favourite, helping the formwork joiners. I was later to do this full-time for many years. The building slowly took shape and eventually I thought it best to look for another job. I still popped in to see Norman and Sue to get my fix of laughter, and then popped across to the Lansdowne Hotel to see Ray and June for more mickey-taking to my own detriment.

One of the lads I worked with on the conference centre asked me if I would come to work with him for a local civil engineering company, and said that I could get a lift there with him near the King's Gambit Café (now long closed) on St. Marychurch Road. On Monday morning I was there bright and early. I got to meet my new boss Brian Binton, and I worked for him for the following three years. The main focus of Brian's work was constructing large industrial steel-framed buildings with all of the associated drainage and power floated flooring. The work was spread out in a 50 mile or so radius from Torquay, but mostly we worked in Totnes, Dunkeswell Aerodrome and sometimes the clay collieries in Dartmoor. After you had been working in the clay collieries, your clothes were good for nothing. That fine white clay would get in so deep it would be impossible to wash out.

Brian was a fantastic boss, and treated me well. I earned a good living, I learned a lot from him, and eventually even set out buildings on my own – but the work remained the same. And that is okay, if that's what you want, but I wanted more. I had a thirst to learn. I kept up my studies at the college and I really enjoyed that part of my life, but I loved the construction industry, the characters you meet, the stories you heard and how comradely everyone is. Even years on I still meet and recognise people from different sites all over the country – there are way too many sites and way too many people to mention. It's a small industry, and wherever you go in the country, you will either recognise someone that you have previously worked with, find out when talking to someone that they know people you know, or meet someone who has worked on the same jobs as you in the past. It really is a small world.

My last job in Torquay was building a new McDonalds on Union Street. The big new shopping centre was just starting to be built at that time, but the subcontractor from Birmingham was paying £20 a day more at the McDonalds site, so I took the job. I was well used to the work sequence at that time, and the building was piled like the conference centre. It was steel-framed with concrete decked floors and an all power float finish to the concrete, so to me it was easy. I think the fact that I could power-float and was good at it was what got me the job. I eventually left Torquay and went to work in Birmingham with the contractor.

When I arrived in Birmingham, I went to live in Small Heath on Heather Road. I spent many years there before moving to Solihull, where I now live. I worked for Andy Finnley, who had quite a lot of men working for him at that time. I wanted to work as a formwork joiner, as I had had my fill of ground-working, concreting and such like. Andy was a big Irish man with even bigger lungs. He was from County Roscommon and was proud of it. I worked for him for some time, and learned a lot about formworks and concrete framed buildings, but eventually it was time to move on and work for other contractors – it was time to learn more. I really liked and respected Andy, he was a good boss, very fair, and I liked his sense of humour. One incident with him that sticks in my mind took place when I was working on a job at the East Birmingham Hospital, now Heartlands.

The job itself was nearly finished. There was quite a lot of stone and rubbish left over from drainage works that we had done in one of the courtyards, and all of this material had to be moved out by the coming Friday, as a separate blockwork contractor was starting work on the location on Monday morning.

Andy characteristically took to a high spot where he could see his workers, shouting orders at them from his vantage point. There was a 360° track digging machine working, loading a six-ton dumper with stone to take away out of the courtyard and to another part of the job. The driver of the dumper was an old Irish guy called Chris Finnegan – Chris was a bit of a character and a bit of a drinker. It was a hot summer's day, and Chris kept getting off the dumper on his return to dig up a pile of sand where he'd left a two litre plastic bottle of cider. He buried it to keep it cool and away from the sun.

Andy had spotted Chris's antics from his vantage point, waited for him to leave on the dumper and started bellowing out orders to me from his high spot…

'Hoy, hoy. Hey Brummie, you'll move the bottle – you will?'

I looked up, and shrugged my shoulders with a look of bemusement on my face. 'Move the bottle – you will?'

'Move the bottle, you thick Brummie! Back he's coming, hurry on ta fuck up, will ya?' He blasted this out while expertly puffing on his fag.

'Ah, I see – sorry Andy.'

'You'll be fuckin' sorry all right. Hurry on, Brummie – back he's coming…'

I removed the two litre plastic bottle of cider, and placed it in a hole on the opposite side of the sand. Sure enough Chris Finnegan returned on his dumper for another load of stone, got off and proceeded to dig in the sand for his bottle of cider. Well, Chris dug like a rabbit, with his two hands acting as shovels, firing out sand between his legs.

'Hee haw, heeee haw,' Andy shouted with the palms of his hands on the sides of his head to represent donkey ears. 'Heeee haw. For fuck's sake, that's cat. Dat is fucking cat altogether. Hee haw, heeee haw, heeeeee… Cat, dog, fuckin cat…' There were tears of laughter rolling down his fat red face.

Chris dug and dug until he found his bottle, then he laid it flat in the sand before taking it to his mouth. His head was scarlet, his forehead covered in sweat and the bottle was caving in with each swig he took, his red cheeks going in and out like bellows as he emptied his two litre plastic bottle of cider. Andy was still shouting obscenities and making 'hee haw' noises from his vantage point. Chris, cool as he was, got up, gave Andy a one-fingered salute and said, 'Fuck you, bollocks', and walked off-site to the pub.

I worked on some really big projects, such as the new Toyota factory at Burniston, Derbyshire and the Supertram in Sheffield. There were some big bridges and other structures that had to be constructed to enable the tram to operate. I was there for ten years, after which I went to Germany to work on hydroelectric structures. I worked in Glauchau, Zwickau and a small village called Thierbach, which are all based around the river Mulde that runs through Saxony in what was formerly East Germany. I loved working in Germany, the people were just so friendly, and I had some great times at people's houses, during nights out and, of course, at the local beer fests. The country itself, so cleanly and hospitable, was just a wonderful place to experience – not to mention that the beer is just divine and second to none.

After two years working in Germany – coming home every eight weeks for the weekend – I'd managed to save enough money to enable me to buy a house. My long-term girlfriend Marie and I were talking about getting married, so I mulled that over for a while. On landing at Birmingham BHX Airport on my last trip home from Germany, I thought I needed a holiday. After discussing where best to go for an eight-week break, Marie told me she was keen on touring America, so I booked a flight to Los Angeles for the following week.

We landed at LAX and got ourselves a hostel for a few days – mainly recovering from the jet lag and acclimatising to the heat. After looking around L.A. we decided to head up to San Francisco via the Pacific Coast Highway, which was about 450 miles or so. It took us about two days as we called at Carmel, and, me being in construction, I also wanted to see the Bixby Bridge. The road was all coastal and full of twists, turns and steep inclines and declines. It was breathtaking. Houses seemed to be perched up high on the hills and clifftops; it must be incredible to live in one of those places, overlooking the ocean, seeing that panorama every morning when you wake up and wander around in a semi-vegetative state, scratching your balls. We stopped off at different vantage points along the way to take in the warm sea air and to just marvel at the beauty of the place. More than keen to see the Bixby Bridge before getting to Carmel, I just wanted to press on and was a hard taskmaster to Marie, but we both wanted to see as much as we could in the eight weeks.

The Bixby Bridge was incredible, spanning a huge gorge at a length of 85 metres and a height of 80 metres. It was something to really marvel at, and to think it was completed in 1932 during the Great Depression – that made it even more incredible and inspiring. Amazing to think the thing was all made of reinforced concrete, and with its remote location, you really appreciate the determination and commitment that went into getting the thing built at that time. What an achievement, what a shining light. Finally, Marie dragged me away kicking and screaming, leaving long fingernail marks on the road, and we headed for Carmel. Carmel was pristine and just like a toy-town. We stayed overnight, had pizza and watched Toy Story, which was amazing, as it was the first time I'd seen animation that good.

After another long stretch, we finally arrived in San Francisco, which was another feast for the eyes – I just wanted to see the Golden Gate Bridge and Alcatraz. We saw them in good time, but the hilly streets, the trollies and the wooden houses just took our breath away completely; I would imagine that anyone would instantly fall in love with San Francisco at first sight. We went down to the harbour to take a boat trip and were both just spellbound by its beauty. We only spent two days there, but I long to return and will never forget how wonderful it was.

Next stop on the way to Las Vegas was the giant redwood trees. At nearly 300 feet high and 20-something feet across, they are the biggest living things and just breathtaking to see. With some of them dating back nearly 3,000 years, they hold a presence, and they are very peaceful, spiritual things indeed – you can feel it. Although they are so massive, you know they are vulnerable, and that one day, like most things, humans will fuck them over. Just like they do everything else in a non-sustainable lust for power to control everything and everyone. Let me tell you right here and now: there will only be one winner in that Russian roulette game, and it won't be humans.

Vegas was also an incredible place, and we wandered around looking at all the gaming and the machines. Of course, we had to get a cup full of quarters and have a go on the slots. Fortunately, neither of us won, because we would most likely have continued until we had given it all back and more besides. A helicopter ride to the Grand Canyon for a hundred dollars was a steal, and so off we went over the red sandstone canyon, marvelling at the tones of colour of the stone, water and sky. It takes you to another world, and the feast for your eyes is something you cannot ever erase from your mind – not that you would ever want too. I wanted to go to the Hoover Dam and see the Barringer Meteor Crater in Coconino County, but I was okay with missing out on them. We had to press on too see more stuff.

Off we went to our next stop, Houston. We only stayed overnight as we were both keen to get to New Orleans to listen to the music and wander around the French Quarter. We stayed there about two days, and the music was phenomenal – there were solo singers and ten piece bands – ranging from blues to bluegrass and country. It was jumpin'. The architecture of the French Quarter, with the ornate cast-iron pillars, columns and balconies, was outstanding. We pressed on and planned to head north, but first we had to visit the Alamo on the Rio Grande. This place also had deep history and you could feel the struggle that went on there.

Finally, we made our way up to Nashville, bar hopping from place to place, listening to more class music at as many venues as possible. The music there is second to none. Of course no visit to Nashville would be a visit to Nashville without going to The Grand Ole Opry. The atmosphere on the way into the place was something to hold – those American women knew how to dress, with those white cowboy boots and white leather jackets covered in tassels and rhinestones. My ribs were sore from Marie's nudges, pokes and thumps, but I couldn't help but look. The atmosphere in the

Grand Ole Opry is incredible, and like no other venue on earth.

Next stop was Memphis for more music, and also to go to Graceland to see the King's house. I thought I'd find a happy vibe there, but, although it was astonishing, it was also sad. The tones of Elvis came into your head, and seeing those family graves, as beautiful as they were, with the noise of the water, couldn't help but make you feel so sad. Such a talented person taken away by the Good Lord so early in his life and career.

The highlight of our tour was over, and we travelled on to Chicago, to Buffalo, Niagara Falls and of course New York. From New York we went to Washington, then back through the Grand Canyon on a ground-level, spent another two days in Vegas and then went to San Diego to chill for a week before getting our return flight to the UK from Los Angeles.

Back in the UK, I took a week off before looking for work as a carpenter. I soon found a job, which demonstrates the real beauty of the construction industry: you can simply meet a few lads in the local pub, find out who's hiring and just turn up early on Monday morning with your tools and working gear on. And, if all else fails, you can just wander from site to site until you do get something. People would never be out of work as long as they didn't spend their days in the pub, or miss shifts on a regular basis. I did neither – but sometimes culture dictated that I had to spend most of the afternoon in the pub with the foreman or subcontractor boss.

The work was hard on those sites. You were either stuck down in a big hole filled with putrid air from diesel engines or calicoes dust from general works, or out in the open with the weather beating you down. The heat in those deep excavations was incredible, and it would just be absorbed into the concrete, escalating the temperature even further. On top of that there was no air flow, and no escape from the prison camp mentality of the work bosses looking down on you all day, shouting orders at you. I'm sure they all got a kick out of it, and I bet most had a fuckin' hard on. There were occasions when I'd run up the ladder and go nose to nose with some dickhead foreman to put him straight. Mainly I was left alone as I was a good worker, but I did what I had to do if someone was getting on my wick. The work was heavy and hard, and the shifts were often 10 or 12 hours long. I mostly worked six days a week, sometimes seven.

The pay was good, but nothing near what it should have been to compensate for the short life expectancy or for the mental stress I endured. There were not many who stuck it out, and there were few that made it past 60 years of age. Some good fit lads bowed out and died in their early 40s – that is no age to die from the burden of work. They don't put these occupational deaths down as statistics, but maybe they should think about doing it. Invariably on inner city jobs there would be no parking for the workers – only for the office staff only. I wondered how long they would last if they had to hump their heavy bag of tools and work clothing down the street, and then up the stairwell of a concrete framed building. Tears and blisters would see the back of them before the day was out, I reckon.

Eventually I found a house I wanted to buy. It was in Hay Mills, Birmingham, on Deakins Road. The house was a repossession, and was heavily gutted and rundown inside. After spending weeknights and all my weekends doing the place up from top to bottom, Marie and I decided on a date and place to get married. I sold the house in Hay Mills, making a small profit, and we moved to a new place just off the Swan Island at Yardley. Everyone in Birmingham knows the Swan Island – it used to be the location of the Swan Public House, first established in 1605, which was once the biggest pub in England. Interestingly, I worked on the new office block that was built on the old footprint of the Swan Pub. After another total house refurbishment, we later moved to a house in Solihull where we settled.

Suspicion and Nudges

Marie and I got married at a church in Small Heath Birmingham on the 5th of September, 1998. I was 33 years of age and Marie was two years younger. Marie was from a well-established family, and had close relatives living all over Birmingham and the rest of the UK. Her mother and father were both Irish, and had broad accents; they were both from County Donegal and had moved from Ireland to the UK in the mid-1950s. They met in Birmingham, and married two years later. They bought a house in Small Heath, raised four kids and had still been living there together until just recently. Marie's father died in 1995 at 83, and her mother was to later move house in early 2016. What an upheaval it must have been for her after living in the same house for 56 years – leaving a house full of memories, of birthdays, weddings and family occasions. Good job a house is only bricks and mortar and you can take all of those memories with you in your head. But nevertheless, even with that in mind, it still probably wasn't easy for her to swallow. Marie's mum just wanted to move into a bungalow, to make things easier for her in her advancing years. She also wanted to be closer to her two daughters and one of her sons – her older son lived in London, and she wanted room for him to stay when he came to visit.

It was a big wedding. Well, on Marie's side. I of course had no family, and it made me feel very vulnerable and at best inadequate. It took some balls, I can tell you, and instead of feeling happy about the whole thing, I felt exposed, helpless and somehow fraudulent. I have to thank the McGinley family for welcoming me into their fold, but some things I hadn't quite accounted for were soon to test my morale and confidence to the max. The bride's family sat on one side of the church and the groom's family sat on the other side. Of course Marie, with her huge extended family, had a packed-out side of the church – and it was quite clearly overflowing – so some of her family stood at the side and at the back of the church, anything but to fill up my side which had no one seated in the pews apart from me and my best man. *This is the most unnerving feeling imaginable*, I thought.

As I sat and waited for Marie to enter the church I couldn't help but think about the family I knew I must have, that should be sat their filling the empty pews behind me. In this moment of solidarity, support came from my friend Gary, who got up from Marie's side and came to sit on his own on my side of the church. He was shortly followed by his now wife Maria. Trickling over from Marie's side of the church to mine came people that I'd worked with, drank with and socialised with. The number of people on my side of the church kept rising as more came to support me. Then I felt accepted, I felt their support and love for me, and I was content to get married.

The organ pumped out 'Mendelssohn's Wedding March' and eventually Marie came through the church doors with her father proudly holding her arm. I really don't know who was proudest at that moment: me or Marie's father. The music, the ambiance and the flowers... It just seemed to be heavenly and surreal. I had to of course face the front as best I could, but I also had to turn to look with everyone else in the church. Eventually Marie was standing by me, and her father gave her away and went to sit next to Marie's mother. The ceremony seemed to last a lifetime, but went quick at the same time – how strange, what a crazy feeling. After all of the speeches and the 'you may now kiss the bride', there was deafening applause. I was overwhelmed and just kept thinking that I didn't deserve all the love and attention. We then turned to walk up the petal-strewn isle to the sound of a group of hired singers singing 'Ave Maria'. It made me cry.

Outside the church on that bright summer's day, we stood and enacted various poses for the photographer. My best man and I went off around the church grounds and the flower garden to have different pictures taken, then it was Marie and the bridesmaids' turn and then me and Marie's turn. By this stage I was worn out already, and wondered when it would stop. We finally got into the wedding cars only to be taken on a detour to another garden with flowers and trees. Petals were thrown about on the grass and more pictures were taken. 'You stand there', 'kneel', 'stand with him', 'stand with those'... And to think that we were paying the chump. But it was all worth it in the end as the pictures turned out brill.

We got back into the wedding cars and headed off up to the reception which was at the Emerald Club in Bordesley Green, Birmingham. This is when I felt really uncomfortable on account of my upbringing; I was just waiting for that tap on the shoulder, someone saying, 'Come with me, son,' and then getting beaten, mentally tortured and probably felt up by some pervert member of staff. I was just getting the vibe that people were thinking, *Who's he? Where did he come from? Does anyone know anything about him?* I couldn't prove anything, because I didn't know anything much about myself or my own history – it was a big jumbled mess – but most of what I did think turned out to be true anyway.

Marie and I stood in the doorway of the wedding reception venue, shook people's hands and thanked them for coming from near and far, before eventually making our way up to the top table. Again, here I felt even more exposed – there was no escape from it all. There was Marie's family at one side of the table, and just little ol' me on my side representing 'what bloody family?' This was through no fault of my own, my past followed me everywhere, and it exposed me and made me feel like crap. But for that day I was going to bluff it out, and try to ignore my ghosts and prevent the daemons from poking me as I sat in front of Marie's extended family and my friends.

All of the people sat down and looked up at the top table. Marie and her sister gave flowers to the bridesmaids, to other members of her family and of course to her mother. It was all very emotional, and very difficult for me to deal with. Finally, it was time: 'Can you all be upstanding for the father of the bride?' Speech, speeeech. Marie's father, God bless, was a working man, and he wasn't a man for the limelight and definitely not one for speeches and ceremonies. And besides, his broad Donegal accent was difficult to understand. He flunked it and was struggling for something to say, so I got up and improvised. I don't know how I did it, but I gave the perfect speech, the perfect spiel. Afterwards I got backslaps, and people telling me what a brilliant speech I had given. I had written nothing down and I was ill prepared, but my heightened state of nervousness, my adrenaline and my bloody 'stand up and be counted' mentality took me through it all.

At the start of my speech I got heckles, then it calmed down and they listened. I thanked people for coming from near and far – especially those who had travelled from abroad – and for taking the time out of their busy schedules and from their work commitments, and for making arrangements in their absence. I said that we would do our best to ensure that the second half of their day would be every bit as good as the first. I thanked Marie's family for accepting me into theirs; I put it to them that I had no family of my own, and that I had been brought up in council care homes, children's homes and by foster parents. I said that they were now my new family if they accepted me. The guests were in the palm of my hand, and there was total silence but for the few people that were crying.

I thanked Marie's sister's family for supplying the cars, all who had given flowers and all who had attended, and then I turned my attention to the management team of the Emerald Club, thanking them for what a professional job they had done with the decoration and the presentation of the tables. Then I went on to say, 'I hope you all have a wonderful day. Marie and I are so privileged to have such fantastic family and friends, enough to make anyone else truly envious. Charge your glasses and please be upstanding for the McGinley family.' I will never know where it all came from, but it flowed like slurry out of my mouth. You could have grown the finest of roses in that bullshit.

At the end of the meal, it was time for the band to strike up for the first dance. We had been practicing a little, but I was rubbish – I had two left feet big-time. The limits of my dancing skills were erratically bouncing around to punk, ska, acid house and reggae music whilst completely out of my tree on Red Stripe lager and testosterone. I was clearly embarrassed to the inch of my life, but slowly sympathisers joined in around us. This made things a whole lot better before I was able to make a sharp exit away from the dance floor and to the relative safety of my friends, who were smoking outside in peace. I would only smoke after I'd had a good drink, or a sharp shock, and that's still the case today – although sometimes I don't bother with fags even when polluted with drink.

I left Marie bopping on the dance floor to do the mingling thing, and I soon realised that the same old questions were coming out of everyone's mouths – the mouths of people I trusted and respected. The alcohol was loosening their tongues, and their undercover subtle gestures were becoming more pronounced and their abjection towards me more and more apparent as the night went on. The questions were quite understandable and justifiable from concerned friends and the relatives of Marie. Though they already knew the answers, they prodded and poked in the hope that they would find holes in my story, comparing and contrasting the results amongst themselves, adding two and two together to make 546.

When you marry, you receive questions and mistrust, and are degraded by your partners' siblings and parents. The initial succinct questions are bad enough, and if you get past that stage and are accepted, despite being brought up in a cruel environment – which you never had any choice over in the first place – then the real questions start. The family almost think they own you. You are almost a pet, a talking point, a freak show. You are continuously undermined and never ever truly accepted or deemed acceptable. You are questioned and re-questioned about holes in your story – which people in general can never understand – and they begin to think your story is just an excuse, a big fat lie. The human mind runs riot. They convince themselves that you've done something bad in your life, and that you are not even reasonably adequate for their friend, daughter or sibling in their eyes. Their blatant, backwards short-sightedness knows no bounds. The worst questions are the wordless ones: the stares, the glances, the pure disdain in their poisonous, grimacing lour and body language. All of it is unnerving, intolerable and continually undermining.

On top of all this, there is the cold, cold fact that you don't know your own past yourself, because you have no evidence of what it was like. No aunt, uncle, mother, father, sibling or cousin to say, 'Remember when I...?' or 'Remember when we went to...?' You see, there is no point of reference, no yard stick, and therefore you do not know to a point what did or did not happen in the past. All you remember are the awful things, all the negative stuff, which takes a lifetime to work its way out of your system. Help received from do-gooder social workers tortured me, with them asking generic, unfeeling, perverse questions like: 'Did they touch you?'

So bloody ironic when the adults are supposed to be vetted when put into these positions of power.

Yet on my wedding day of all days, the perverse questions kept coming from those 'fur-coat, no-knickers' types of people, who I am sure are whiter than white themselves, who are in fact perfect manifestations of bullshit itself. Those hungry, nosey people continued to pry slyly from different angles, trying to enter my defences in ways other than the portcullises with the murder holes above. But they could only get the answers I had, so in the end they had to scurry back to their huddle – or vipers' nest – to concoct some other line, twisting, scowling and stinking of whiskey and cigarettes.

Although I was quite used to the question and answer sessions, and was highly trained – apprenticed into it almost – those questions kept coming and I was glad when it was time to leave the Emerald Club and to go to honeymoon suite at the Copthorne Hotel in Birmingham.

We got up the next day and made our way to Marie's parents' house in Small Heath to look at all of the cards, well-wishing gifts, flowers and notes. They had all been sorted out and placed for us to look at in the front room. We sat there for a while, sifting through all of the gifts and cards, and consuming copious amounts of strong tea and the odd sandwich – which you dare not refuse in an Irish household. Mrs Doyle of the programme *Father Ted* on Craggy Island springs to mind: 'Ah, go on. Go on, go on, go on.' And so it really does go on until you just say 'ok then,' and eat the blooming sandwich, drink the drink or whatever it may be. All of the time I was sitting there, I had that 'sacred heart' picture looking at me. No matter where you were in that room, no matter how obscure, I swear those eyes would always look straight at you. I myself am not a religious person, but I really do believe that someone watches over us. The different routes we are made to take in life and the stumbling blocks we face are designed to test our wills. To my mind, there cannot be any other explanation for what happened to me, and for how I survived at all.

Eventually we got a taxi to Birmingham BHX and flew out to Halkidiki in mainland Greece for our honeymoon, and two weeks after that it was back to Birmingham to get on with life. Marie had been working as a care assistant in local care homes, doing the odd bank shift for extra cash. It was hard work and the pay was poor. She was flogging a dead horse with trying to work extra shifts, and I noticed that she wasn't holding out well mentally. I tried to keep a lid on Marie's failing mental health and carried on as if it wasn't a problem, hoping that the symptoms would slowly abate. I hoped that she was just adjusting to married life and being away from her family. That would be understandable, I thought.

One evening we went to dinner at a friend's house. There were about nine of us in total, and our hosts Gary and Maria had cooked a lovely Thai green curry. Two of Marie's close cousins were there, and we drank and ate our way through all of the courses including dessert. It was clear to me that Marie wasn't coping well at all, but the others couldn't quite see it and probably thought she had had too much to drink. We were playing Jenga and when it came to Marie's turn she was shaking uncontrollably. Of course she received heckles and took it personally – though she had a nervous kind of demeanour, so people knew when to lay off. When it came around to Marie's turn again, she just swiped at the pile of Jenga bricks to the horror of everyone on the table – although it was a relief to me at the time, because the cat was out of the bag. I knew it was 'a problem halved is a problem shared' situation at that point. I thought I could cope and keep her condition under wraps but it just wasn't happening. I was buckling under the strain of trying to handle and contain Marie's mental illness.

Marie then proceeded to throw Jenga bricks at each individual Jenga player. She was upset and thought that they were all ganging up on her, singling her out and bullying her – but, of course, this was not the case. Marie, who was later diagnosed as a paranoid schizophrenic, just could not see that at the time. It is a really frightening illness for those who come in contact with it, not to mention for the person who is affected. The stigma attached to this illness was still very medieval-like, even though Marie was perfectly harmless, and nonviolent. She did see and hear things – voices, noises, and who knows what else – but all everyone else saw was 'paranoid schizophrenic', and in their minds there were images from the Norma Bates shower scene from the film *Psycho*. So with visions like that in their minds, along with ducking stools and people being burnt at the stake, people drifted away, making lame excuses not to call to the house. 'Oops, I'm sorry, I forgot to invite you two' – yeah, right, whatever. None of this helped Marie's condition and only fuelled and justified her increasing bouts of paranoia.

Marie's close cousin Mickie enveloped her in his arms, and tried to console her while she cried hysterically. Mickie looked at me with a confused, frightened look. There was also a knowingness in his eyes, and at that moment my trust in her family waned. I knew that he had known about Marie's illness, I knew that Marie's mother, father and siblings had known and I also knew that Marie herself had known about it. They had hatched a whole conspiracy on how to hide it from me. I had been so wrapped up in wanting a loving family all of my life that I had ignored all of the signs. I wasn't slow when it came to deciphering people – I could usually suss anyone out fairly quickly – but I had been well and truly stitched up and betrayed. I felt my heart sink, and from then on our marriage went downhill. The deal was off, but I couldn't leave Marie like that. None of it was her fault, and I hung on for years until doctors found the medicine that suited her and made her well again. She was dependant on pills, but cured all the same.

After the night at Gary and Maria's house, Mickie arranged for me to meet him somewhere to discuss Marie's condition. We met in a local pub, and the questions came loaded toward me – Mickie just wasn't accepting that his close cousin was ill. But there was one thing wrong: his eyes were lying. I eventually got him to admit that he and the family had known Marie was ill for a long time. She had been diagnosed with depression at the age of 15, and I suspect that her mother, father and siblings had always known something wasn't quite right with her.

After I met with Mickie, I had clandestine meetings with Marie's two brothers, both separately. After receiving a barrage of questions aimed at me as to what had happened to Marie – 'she was fine before she met you', etc. – I finally got the truth out of each brother in turn... Marie had always been mentally ill. Marie's sister never initiated any form of contact, she hated me from the start, and I called and asked several times if she would meet me to discuss my concerns about Marie. She refused point-blank each time. Marie's mother wouldn't discuss it either, as she had a 'put her in the attic and don't let anyone know' attitude, a total refusal to accept failure. Any mention of Marie's failings was seen as an attack on the family, but closing ranks was probably the worst thing the family could have done for Marie's mental health. You can only move on if you accept people's failures, and learn and progress; find a solution by hook or by crook. But the family encircled the wagons and there was no getting in.

As time went on in our marriage, things got progressively worse. She was convinced she was being watched by someone, everyone, and that the TV was giving her messages. The people on the TV were talking directly to her, and there was a camera in the TV through which she was being watched. You name it, she imagined it.

One time, when she was having a particularly bad night, I woke up to find her ranting and in a mess. She called her sister, Jackie, who was utterly drunk started shouting down the phone and blaming me for everything that had happened to Marie, saying I made her how she was. I had to grab the phone and try to talk to Jackie, to tell her that her sister was frightened to death, that she was seeing armed men in the room, and that she needed comfort from her mum or her sister. Jackie, who finally saw the seriousness of the whole situation, promised Marie that she would be there first thing in the morning to take her to her mother's house. Jackie never admitted to me, and probably not even to herself, that Marie had always been ill. At least her two brothers had the decency to come clean. I thank them and Mickie both for that, as I badly needed as much support as I could get at that time.

The next day, a very agitated Marie waited for hours for Jackie to pick her up and take her to her mum's. Of course, she never came and I was left with a terrified wife on the cusp of a nervous breakdown. She would rock backwards and forwards while she sat, and, as she stood, she would dance from side to side, moving back and forth from one foot to the other, with both her arms going backwards and forwards. Her eyes seemed to change colour to a deep satanic black, with the pupils dilating. I, who am not usually frightened, was scared to death.

After numerous phone calls to her mum, it was decided that I would take Marie down to her house. I had a small Citroen van and, after much negotiation, I persuaded Marie to come with me so that I could drop her off at her mother's house.

I got Marie outside and we made our way to the van. I opened the door and she darted back into the house. I asked her what was the matter, and she explained to me that there were armed men waiting for her in my van. I can tell you it scared me, and I really didn't know what to do, but eventually Marie agreed to take the bus with me. We went across the road and waited, but no bus came. We'd perhaps only waited five minutes – though it seemed like hours – and this was enough to convince her that the bus had been held up by the police, with armed men changing into civilian clothes in order to pounce on her when she got on board. She ran back into the house, and it took an hour before she let me in. Neighbours on our cul-de-sac were out, looking, pointing and talking in groups. This of course only added to Marie's paranoia. I couldn't go over and tell them to mind their own business, or even explain my predicament, as it would only heighten Marie's suspicion.

Eventually I got Marie to open the front door and managed to talk her down enough to get her to phone her mother – I thought she might be able to calm her down. After a long telephone call, and some very gentle persuasion, I finally got Marie to leave the house and tried to get her on the bus again. There was still no sign of her sister Jackie, who had a people carrier with blacked out windows because she thought she was famous. In reality she was a five-foot-two fat dwarf. We had boarded the bus at last, and still had about four miles to go, when we saw people we knew. I motioned for them to leave us alone, which further convinced Marie there was a conspiracy. She saw her chance and broke free from the bus at the Swan Island in Yardley, Birmingham. From there she walked all of the way to her mother's house in Small Heath.

On arriving at her mother's house, Marie was met by her curtain-twitching mum, who rushed to open the front door, more for fear that the neighbours would see Marie than for the health and wellbeing of her daughter. As for me, I didn't factor into the equation at all – after all I was only a bastard kid who had been practically manipulated into marrying and caring for her daughter.

The door opened and a petrified Marie was practically pulled inside the house by her neighbour-conscious mother. Marie's mother gave bitter, venomous instruction to me – 'Say nothing, tell nobody' – and slammed the door shut, letting her words ring out. There I stood outside Marie's mother's house in Small Heath, gobsmacked at the treatment I had received. I'd had no proper sleep for days on account of Marie's nocturnal paranoia, and still had to work twelve hour shifts in order to bring in a wage. I couldn't believe the sheer ignorance of Marie's family, their damned point-blank refusal to admit that Marie was ill. Heaven forbid that anyone should mention or discuss it! And of course this lead to her downfall, and compounded her illness even further. I didn't stand a chance against those bigoted backwards people. Marie herself didn't stand a chance either, against their archaic 'the earth is still flat and dinosaurs never existed' mentality. Well I suppose those hypocrites were dinosaurs themselves, after all I never saw their feet outside of their shoes to prove otherwise – sorry, hooves.

Dismayed and exhausted, I walked straight to the George & Dragon Pub on Coventry Road. I needed a drink to calm my nerves. After half-a-dozen shots of whiskey, I waited outside and got the bus back home to my little dog Jess. Strange, but the dog seemed to have more bloody sense than all of Marie's family put together. We also had a Persian cat called George, who had brown owl-like eyes – causing him to just looked bewildered all of the time – and even he had more cop than Marie's bigoted, blinkered family. I don't think any of them, close or extended, would recognise that Marie was ill at close range, let alone at 20 paces. They saw Marie's obvious illness as a personal attack on their family, instead of a learning, helping opportunity. The skeletons were well and truly out of the cupboard and would never go back in no matter how much they willed it. The next day I went back to work as normal. I didn't see Marie again for six weeks, and none of her family contacted me to let me know if she was okay. None of them called around to ask how I was coping, to check if I was feeling okay, or even to find out how my own mental health was holding up. It wasn't good actually, if you are reading – not good at all.

One day Marie and her mum turned up at our house, acting just as if the event had never occurred. Marie still did her dance, she still looked very unwell, and I was asked to make sure that she took her new pills. Now, if you ever have to make sure that a paranoid schizophrenic takes their pills, believe me, you have got a job on your hands. She was convinced I was trying to poison her. Stopping Marie from hiding pills under her tongue, hiding them on the roof of her mouth and substituting them for other ones wasn't half of the story. It was a challenge, but she started getting better with each one she took. We laugh about it now, but at the time it really took its toll on us both.

Sometimes Marie didn't sleep for days on end, her eyes a deep demonic black, and I knew she was about to have another episode. Then I wouldn't see her for weeks, and she'd remain at her mother's house. It was really difficult knowing that I was married to a bottle of pills instead of a real person. She was a drug-manipulated being, and it would take years for her to start getting her innate humour back – about ten years to be more precise. Marie subsequently had over a year off work due to her illness, and as a result, and quite understandably too, she nearly lost her job. She had to go in to work for meetings on her future with the NHS – it was a demanding time to say the least. Even though my wages were our only form of income, I really needed to be off work with her. I had as much time off as I could, and when it came to getting a new contract I dragged my feet. Realistically, she should have had full-time care. But instead she just stewed in her own juices in the house alone most of the time, with only Jess and George for company, and the occasional visit from her mother. Her poisonous sister never visited.

One very cold winter's day, Marie walked out of the house convinced I was trying to lure her into the arms of the people that wanted to take her away. Well, she took off her coat, because it had listening devices and small tracking devices sewn into it, and then moved on to the rest of her clothes. With armfuls of her clothing, I followed her all the way to her mother's in Small Heath. Despite the fact that it was a freezing cold winters day, Marie had beads of sweat on her forehead. Her eyes were also as black as coal. She walked a far faster pace than she would normally, and seemed to have the strength of a shire horse. Once again, I didn't see her for weeks on end and received no explanation, not that I expected one. This cycle went on, and I got more and more beaten down… But I carried on. After all I had been through in life, I wasn't about to give up on Marie just yet, and I wasn't going to let her Neolithic-minded family beat me.

The general public are great at coming to conclusions. I went out with Marie on numerous occasions, and she could drink a lot, being of Irish descent. Occasionally she would get paranoid and just burst into tears. She would see things and assume that people were looking at her and talking about her. Then people would step in and sometimes try to punch me, push me away and call me a bully. You really couldn't make it up, but at the same time you really couldn't blame the public for assuming things either. I've been out with friends and Marie has just burst into tears and wanted to get out of the venue. This was embarrassing at times, but our friends kind-of got used to it after some time. They knew I wasn't to blame and could see themselves that Marie was harmless but very ill.

I have to say, at this point, I did receive a lot of help at the latter end of my marriage, but it was way too late – the damage was done and I had failed her. I just couldn't take it any longer, I wasn't strong enough, but I challenge anyone not to buckle under those conditions with no allies. If these people would have come forward earlier in my marriage, then I'm sure that their support would have carried me through. Some of Marie's close cousins, including Mickie, finally saw things for what they were – they finally saw that Marie's sister Jackie was a totally selfish, bigoted control-freak who would blame anyone and anything for her younger sister's condition. They finally saw that Marie needed help and not to be chastised and talked down to as though she were a retarded child. I finally got some justice. Marie eventually got well, with the help of medication, by trial and error, finding something that was just tailored to her condition, and now finally she has her sense of humour back. She is still a little bit paranoid at times, but I think we all are and I really don't see that as a bad thing. She works all of her shifts at the NHS, and that in itself is a great achievement for both Marie and for the NHS in supporting her, keeping her job open and being kind and patient.

Marie was treated like a child and like a bad smell – ignored, talked down to, and controlled – something I fully emphasised with. I had severe mental abuse bestowed upon me, and tragically I think Marie's mental trauma and illness was fuelled by the blinkered people who were closest to her. They should have grown a set of bollocks, admitted their mistakes early on and worked with Marie and myself to deal with her illness. The bigots should have at least given us some support. Also, the bloody neighbours didn't need to know anything – though that said, my god, if they were the only thing I'd had to worry about, then I would've been a happy bunny.

As a result of my upbringing, and being subjected to every kind of abuse imaginable – a lot more than the ordinary person can ever imagine – I am afraid of nothing and no-one. But, I can tell you something: when you are married to a paranoid schizophrenic, sometimes some things really frighten you. I would be in bed asleep and something inside would wake me, and I'd open my eyes and see a shadowy figure. Not knowing if it was an intruder in the house, I would shout and put on the bedside lamp. People are scared of the unknown, so until you can see what has startled you, you cannot get out of your adrenaline-filled state. There she stood, motionless with that dark satanic look in her eyes, staring at me, watching me sleep. I got used to it in the end. I'd wake up to find that she'd pulled up a chair to stare at me, and sometimes her face would be only inches from mine, head tilting from side to side like an inquisitive animal. I can tell you without a shadow of a doubt that being exposed to that would frighten anyone.

Anyway, situations like this one just lead to the start of divorce proceedings. I couldn't do it any longer. In ten years of marriage I never had any washing done, I could count the meals I'd had cooked for me on one hand and I couldn't count one proper conversation. If I came home on a summer's day, the curtains would be closed and Marie would be in bed because she'd practically been up all night, either watching me sleep or trawling the hedgerows with her eyes looking for armed assailants. If she was well, then the curtains would be open on occasion, but never before midday and never fully open – always about a foot wide at most. She would never air the place by having a window or door open, and she would never tidy up, wash up or clean in any way. I could always tell when her mother had been around, because the place was hoovered, cleaned and tidied. The woman had been desperate to get Marie married off, so was it any wonder that I was courted and accepted into the family so willingly? I still see Marie regularly and she is doing fine now. She will no doubt be on medication for some time to come, but as long as she doesn't slip back into her little dance moves, then I'm sure she will be okay. She seems happy at any rate, and that's all I can wish for her.

Gone to the Dogs

I was fast approaching a milestone in how long I'd been on the earth – my 40th birthday was on Saturday the 4th, 2005. I had been married to Marie for six and a half years and I knew her only too well. I knew all of her traits and what to look for in her so I could get her home before she got too paranoid and lost it in public. I would never have agreed to have a birthday celebration, let alone go out specifically to celebrate my 40th birthday. I just wasn't and still am not that sort of person. Basically I haven't got the mentality of a ten-year-old person: 'Yay, it's my birthday. Look Mummy, watch me on the slide, look at my face and legs all covered in chocolate.' No, birthdays are definitely not for me. At the time I worked in heavy civil engineering as a foreman, formwork carpenter and shuttering chippie. It was rough hard work, and you have to be tough to endure it. I take my hat off and salute all of those people in my industry, the civil engineering industry, as it is tough for those unsung people on the ground, out in all weather.

The venue chosen for my 40th birthday was the Hall Green Stadium dog track in Birmingham. There were about 20 of us in total, and we had a sit down meal and made a few bets on the dog races. I don't know many men that won, and it always seems to be the women at either dog or horse races that walk away with bundles of cash. They don't seem to spend their own money, borrowing off their fella, and yet they keep the winnings – sounds like a very good deal to me. Perhaps I have it all wrong, but I don't think so. We had a good time, better than I would have thought anyway, so I was happy. The food and the service in general was very good. Us lads being lads, we got up and stood near the bar, leaving the ladies to powwow, count their winnings that would never see the light of day again and just generally chat pure dung at their tables.

The close of the evening came. The bar closed pretty early at 11pm so everyone seemed okay, though I think it was more through peoples' continued eating rather than their lack of will to get drunk. Marie got a taxi home with some friends, so that took a weight off my brain cells, and, me being me, I went off to get a late drink with a few lads. I was just happy that Marie hadn't got paranoid in front of everyone, although a lot of them knew her condition and basically they just kept away. We all went off to a snooker club in Acocks Green called Frames – now Scanlon's – and stayed for a while before slowly sloping off home in different taxis to different parts of Birmingham. My mind was racing all night – the word 'birthday' just kept making me think of my lost family. I couldn't shake it off at all for the whole evening and night. Again, like with my wedding day, I couldn't help but think my birthday should have been a family thing.

Where is my family? What am I doing with my life? Have I even got a family?

When I finally got home in the wee small hours – despite the fact that I'd had a good ol' drink for myself – I found that I just couldn't shake off the internal questions about what happened to me earlier in my life. I still remembered the letter from my mother that was taken from me at the George Inn and I still remembered the haunting picture of the person I thought was my father. I still had the nightmares of the man with his arms outstretched, looking into my eyes and screaming, with the face of the man in the photograph. Basically, I was well and truly messed up; the images and the nightmares were going around in my head like a washing machine's contents, and on top of all of it I had Marie and her antics at home. It was all taking a big hit on me – it was eating me from the inside out. I had to do something about it all.

Although it had been the best part of 23 years since I had been to the George Inn in Waterhouses, I knew that it was where I had to start from. A mate of mine always says, 'you gotta get up to get down' – meaning you have to get up off your seat to go to the dancefloor and dance – and you really have to get of your backside to get anywhere. There is also no escaping the fact that you have to go right back to the beginning of your life in order to get a proper perspective on things. Of course, I couldn't go right back to the beginning, because I didn't even know if I had a beginning. It wasn't until recently that I ordered my file from social services to find out what it holds, and, at the point of writing this, I still haven't received it. I think it will take about a month to come through by all accounts. I never even thought about ordering my file back then, as, for one, I didn't know that you could. The other main reason for me not doing it was fear – I basically didn't have the strength within me to see what my past held.

I got up on the Monday morning, nose back to the grindstone, and headed off to work. At the time I was working on a large construction site in Wendsfield, Wolverhampton, and, for months earlier, I had been feeling some sort of vibe there, but I didn't know what it was. Later it turned out that until the age of five I had been brought up in that area – there were still relatives of mine that lived there, and I faintly recognised some streets, buildings and landmarks. I felt I'd been there before. It was all a bit déjà vu, but I just couldn't put my finger on it at all – it almost felt like I was going dizzy and about to fall over. The atmosphere was oppressive and uncomfortable, but at the same time comforting and strangely familiar. I was also incarcerated in the notorious children's home called Braybrook after I was taken away from my mother, or rather she was taken away from me, so maybe that's where a lot of my memories came from. I found myself walking up and down the streets and side streets during my break times, and things were clear but not clear… I saw faint images of factory workers in flat caps on bicycles, some with little petrol motors on the back – things kept becoming clearer... Was I going mad? Further and further I walked during my break times, exploring more streets, more alleyways, looking at more buildings, parks and churches.

I was drawn to an old Victorian school building in particular that was no longer a school. Only after doing my research have I realised that it was perhaps where me and mother walked to take my brothers Brian and Stephen to school. But I can tell you at the time, without this hypothesis, the place freaked me out. I went back there on weekends when I wasn't working, and I trawled the cemeteries, up and down the lines of gravestones, looking for the name Lawton. I found a few old graves, but nothing I could relate to. This hunt became all consuming. It burned me, it fuelled me – I knew I had to go all out in my quest to find out what had happened to me.

After working all that week, my mind was racing. I think that Wednesfield was the subconscious catalyst that drove me towards finding my birth family. But before I could do that, I had to do something else first, something I just didn't want to do: I had to try and locate one of the women I despised most of all, only second to the satanic Mrs Davenport... I had to try and locate my foster mother – someone I had not seen or wanted to see for nearly 23 years.

The last place I lived with my foster parents was in a little village in the Peak District called Waterhouses.

They had been the landlord and landlady of the local pub, the George Inn, and so this is where I drove to first. I know it's a small village, but twenty-three years is a long time to be away from anywhere, and I had to get my bearings. I went to where I thought my foster mother's old friend Jean had lived, figuring that whatever had happened to Rose and David, she would know and tell me something. I knew from there that I would be able to uncover something that would help me in my search. Although it was still very early in the morning, the chimney was smoking and so I knew someone was up. I knocked on the door of what I thought was Jenny's house – I had never been there so I wasn't quite sure if it was the right place or not – and was met with an unfamiliar but friendly face. I asked after Jenny and her husband Stewart, and the lady explained to me that I was in the wrong place and that they lived in a house further down in the village. She told me I couldn't miss it. Now, I am the sort of person that could get lost on a Roman road, but fortunately I made it to the right house on my second attempt.

Five to ten years isn't really enough to change anyone, but when you've not seen someone for twenty-three years they look old – unrecognisable in fact. The door opened and I explained who I was to Jenny. We both cried. I found it difficult to stand and was offered a chair by the wise woman. Jenny made tea, as you do in those situations, and I petted the Jack Russel dogs, who, like all dogs, were excited to see any sort of visitor. Dogs give so much, and although they're unable to utter a single word, they comfort you and make you feel right at home, regardless of your age, abilities, colour, race or creed. We have a lot to learn from them. Jenny came shuffling towards me with a teapot, milk jug, some cups and a sugar bowl on a tray. Then we sat and we talked.

After the wise woman had grilled me and asked me everything but my shoe size, she gave me my foster mother's address. Jenny asked me to not just turn up at her house, but rather phone first to weaken the shock. I thanked Jenny for her help and told her I'd head off back to Birmingham and call my foster mother in a day or two.

I called my foster mother Rose on the Sunday, and we talked for some time. She explained that she was sorry for how she had treated me in the past, and said that she thought she would never see me again. I thought that she had finally repented her actions and saw the error of her ways, but I was wrong. Rose blamed David for her actions, but it takes two to tango and I didn't think for a minute that a person could be lead and steered into abusing a child so easily. Surely their own morals wouldn't let them act in such a way to such a vulnerable young person? There is only one way that people can move forward and that is by admitting to themselves that they were or are wrong. An obstinate Rose just wouldn't acknowledge this thought-process at all, and so deep down I knew she hadn't changed. She just had the wrong bullish attitude towards admitting her own failings. Nevertheless, I reserved judgement, though even after 23 years my thoughts regarding Rose were still very, very raw.

Saying that, even now in the present day, the treatment I received in those council care homes was a lot worse and the thoughts I have about those experiences haunt me on an hourly basis every day. Those cruel bastards. I really don't feel I have to spell out all of the details, because, firstly, I don't think it's fair to expose the reader to such depravities, and secondly, I have not the strength or the will inside me to talk about it. It hurts badly, to think what they did to me and other vulnerable children, and it makes me weak inside. I can only describe it as a feeling of extreme hunger and nausea coupled with the sensation of drowning. That's how I feel every day as I wake up.

Rose explained that she had gotten married and had lived in several places with her new husband, following him around to different construction work sites before they finally settled and retired to Brighton. She spelled it out loud and clear to me that if I came to visit her and Peter, that I was to say that I was her son. I was also to tell no one of my life with her at the George Inn. She explained that she had told people that her son lived with her ex-husband, and had painted a picture to her new friends of her not wanting to take me out of school and university. She went on further to explain that the reason I had never been to visit her in the past was because I was busy with a young family and my own business, and that she and Peter came to see me and their grandchildren to make it easier for me. I took in all of her bullshit and malicious make-belief instructions and reluctantly agreed to her terms. Basically, even at this stage, she was trying to control me from 200 miles away over the phone before I had even met her. I didn't want to see her, but I had to discover the truth of my past.

Brighton Bound

I went to Brighton to visit Rose and her new husband Peter on the following weekend. It took me so long to get to Brighton as I stopped off so many times, wondering whether or not I was doing the right thing and asking myself if I should turn the car around and go back home. Eventually I got to my destination after stopping at every side road to ask for directions; my navigational skills are not the best.

Finally, I got to the front door of Rose's house. My heart sank. I still couldn't believe I was there and I still really didn't want to meet her, but I had to find answers, and my thirst for knowledge trumped my disdain for the woman – one of my tormentors. Finally, I met Rose, my foster mother, and her new husband Peter. I hadn't seen Rose since before I left home at 18 years old, on account of that coward David trying to throttle me. I think I was only 17 when she left David and ran off with Peter. I couldn't leave before then as I was still in council care until the age of 18. They would have locked me up if I had tried to leave before I was 18, and I knew it all too well. I still feel they keep tabs on me now, so maybe Marie is right after all.

After 23 years of not seeing Rose, I thought her demeanour would have changed a little, but she hadn't changed at all. Just as I had picked up from our earlier phone call – it became more apparent in person – she was more worried about me exposing her past web of lies to her new circle of friends than she was excited to see me. So she smiled and welcomed me like the long lost prodigal son. Only I wasn't her son, and I never wanted to be either, but I had to go back to go forward. I had to get up to get down. She was still controlling and she still called me her little bastard – I can't explain how demeaning that was. She knew calling me that was going to hurt me, and she still persisted. Rose looked older and weaker, and had lost her will for games a little; she was chancing her arm, she was no match for me, but I went on playing along with her little charade game. I cannot tell you how it feels to offer love, and only get 'my little bastard' in return. Lovely woman.

This big onstage act in front of Peter filtered away as soon as he left the room and was out of earshot. We chatted quite a lot, and I really wanted to find out about my earlier life, about how I managed to get fostered out to David and Rose, but she kept swerving the subject. She ducked, dived, evaded and shot down every digging question I offered up in an attempt to find out my past. Eventually I found out that Rose was a friend of Mrs Senior, a social worker I used to have. She was the same person that placed me with Mr and Mrs Hood, who used to strap my left hand to the back of a chair in an attempt to force me to write with my right hand. That meant the woman had placed me in the care of unscrupulous people twice to my knowledge, but I wondered how many other times there were. I also found out that I was advertised in the Lichfield Mercury Newspaper – which, if true, made me feel like shit, but I wouldn't have put it past Rose to have concocted the story to have a sly sideswipe at me.

After much tea drinking and hearing about Rose and Peter's achievements, and how brilliant they were, how popular they were and how they had so many friends, I found I'd had enough. I needed to get out of there – I was suffocating from the putrid smell of fear, lies, pretentiousness and aloof, ironic hypocrisy. I only stayed for one day and one night, and that was far more than I could take. I took my little dog Jess with me, a lovely kind-natured little border terrier. I wanted to see her on the seafront – if only the beach had had sand instead of pebbles – and I loved seeing her light up when she got on the beach. Rose loved dogs with a passion, but she couldn't help but shout and snipe at Jess, and call her a little bitch. Even my poor little dog picked up that I was uncomfortable in her presence, even she was unnerved by her and felt scared. Rose even stooped so low as to use poor Jess to get at me, to try and break me, as she could see that nothing else was working. I had faced my fears and overcame my tormentor, and it was now her that was suffocating, even if it was only in that 'on-stage' amateur dramatics way.

Rose asked Peter to take a picture of me to show their so-called friends. Well, that's what she said, but I think it was more to snipe at me. She kept saying that I looked terrible and should do something about myself, such as losing weight or getting my hair cut. I played along with it all and got my picture taken. I was sitting on the sofa with a mug of tea in my hand, and I couldn't raise a smile. I wish I had that picture today, as it was another life changer. I had hit the self-destruct button big-time, and I looked like a whale on the sofa. I'm not a small man normally, but I must have been twenty stone in weight. I was pale and I looked ill – I looked really ill. My eyes were blank, and my expression was shock. Rose, as cutting as she was, recognised that I was a big-time mess. She started being uncharacteristically nice to me, cooking shepherd's pie and all good stuff, but I wasn't at all convinced that their hospitality didn't have other connotations. All control freaks, abusers and bullies withhold the vital information you need to progress in your life. They hold it close to their chests, never relinquishing it fully, only giving you tantalising morsels. This, I believe, is their control. It is the power that they try to exert over you, and it is what gives those sick depraved bastards the attention that they crave.

None the wiser, but glad that I had made a start in my search, having broken down what I now believe to have been the biggest stumbling block in my way to finding out the truth, I got out of bed early the next morning after not sleeping all night. I felt like I was doing a moonlight flit and running away, leaving at about 3am and heading back to Birmingham. My phone rang constantly for days, but I didn't answer it. Eventually I picked up the voicemails left by Rose and heard the genuine worry in her voice as she begged me to contact her, to let her know that I was well. I eventually returned her calls, and from time to time I go down to Brighton to see Rose and Peter. She likes to tell everyone her son is coming to see her. I look at the floor when she says to her friends, 'This is my lad', because they know that I'm not, and I can tell from the way they look at me. But it remains unspoken. It is something for them to talk about, I reckon – something for them to devour whilst pretending to be friends with Rose and Peter. When they ask if I'm glad to see my mum, or say that my mum looks happy to see me, again, I just look at the floor; I cannot bear it. They know all right. I win on that one – I now win.

After returning from the visit to my foster mother and her new husband, I realised I'd taken the first difficult steps towards rehabilitation. The hurt and mistreatment I had received during the years I spent with David and Rose, in different children's homes, in different foster homes… I felt like I was finally beginning to confront everything that had happened to me in the past.

Microfiche and Researcher

A few years passed me by after the first time I went down to see Rose and Peter. I took Marie down to see them once and she thought that they were lovely people. The on-stage act worked wonders with her, but fortunately I knew what lay beyond the backdrop curtain. Mine and Marie's divorce proceedings were pressing on, and finally I got the decree nisi through the post, followed by my decree absolute about four weeks later. I was finally divorced, and it really felt like a weight had been lifted off my mind, and my body also felt as though it had been transformed into a weightless mass. I did still care for Marie, and still do, but I realised that I'd done all that I could in our marriage. I think we both felt that I'd given all that I could morally, mentally and physically. The physical strain really took its toll in the form of weight gain, mental depression, grey hair, and an inherited haggard, lost, sunken look.

I signed over the house to Marie – we are still good friends – and I walked away with my life, although I was still a few drops short of a piss by that stage. I was close to suicide a few times, and I had been to the doctor for anti-depressants more than once, where once again I went through the routine question and answer sessions of the generic forms from the doctor's PC screen. Before my divorce I had close friends coming to me and advising me that I needed to get out of my marriage for my own wellbeing. They informed me of how they had seen me failing in demeanour and health – falling from a fit bright-eyed man into a fat grey-haired wreck. I received support from so many different people. Just when you think that you are going mad, the light shines through the darkness again – it never fails to give justice. The old saying, 'every cloud has a silver lining', is so true and apt.

It is at this point that I must say the solicitor that conducted the divorce had the tact of a lead brick, and the writing abilities of someone sat in a high chair getting fed by Mummy. We lost count of the numerous times we picked the solicitor's toys up when neither Marie nor I would play ball with her contorted images of a catfight divorce scenario – which she concocted because she wanted to milk every last bean out of us. She saw an opportunity in our weakness, but in the end thankfully Marie and I had an amicable divorce. Personally, neither of us could cope with it being any more drawn out than it needed to be, and so it was kept simple: we both talked and both replied to all of the mail promptly. This not only completely pissed off the solicitor, but also Marie's horrible, bigoted sister Jackie, who tried her utmost to interfere with our marriage and our subsequent divorce. But she was strictly kept out of the equation by her mother and brothers who eventually recognised that we had both done all we could in our marriage. Justice at last, but not without so much pain. Though it was nearly worth it just to see Marie's porky tennis ball-shaped sister, the Oompa-Loompa, lose her grip on our marriage.

In divorcing Marie, I lost my surrogate family and as a result, I felt a need to fill the void left by them. The divorce lessened the urgency of my research, as I really needed to sort out my thoughts. Although during my break from research, I still had this feeling building up inside of me that I really needed to do something about my situation and look for my biological family. Firstly, I really needed to recuperate by giving myself some 'me' time. I also by this stage knew that it was just me and only me that could initiate research and come out of the woodwork, or stand up to the plate as it were. I needed to swallow my pride, be proactive and find my family if I had one. And if I didn't, then I'd find out the truth behind my injustice. I really didn't know how to start going about all of it, but I knew how to lock myself away and hide from the world for a while, and so that's what I did. I really would have been quite happy at that point if I didn't see another living soul for the rest of my life. If the whole human race were like my little doggie Jess then I would have had no problems with people at all – as I said, we have a whole bunch of stuff to learn from our loving animals. First things first: I had to find somewhere to live.

Finding a house to rent proved more difficult than I had imagined, and the letting agencies wanted to know everything but my shoe size. Again, it was all bloody questions and answers. I viewed quite a few properties, and finally settled on a little two-bedroom Victorian terrace house on Preston Road in Yardley, Birmingham. One of my first thoughts as I climbed the stairs with the landlord was how gloomy and tired the house seemed. I looked up at the loft hatch in the ceiling at the top of the stairs and thought, 'That's a decent height to jump out off of with a rope tied around my neck.' I was in a total mess; my mental health was not in good shape at all. In hindsight I should have moved further afield to lessen the chances of me coming into contact with nosey question-asking people from the area I knew only too well.

When anyone gets divorced – or even splits up from a relationship for that matter – things previously taken for granted can become very awkward. After a relationship or marriage has ended, your acquired mutual friends as a couple, dual friendships, are put under strain. Each friend holds their own individual alliances, views and opinions on your past relationships. As a very opinionated young man, a schoolteacher once told me, 'Opinions are like arseholes and should never be aired in public', and there is no truer statement. The only other statement to that effect that I found to be very apt and similar is: 'Opinions are all well and good for the employed person, but can easily lead to them becoming an unemployed person with opinions.'

After a divorce, you have to shield yourself from this kind of exposure, and find out who your friends are and who you are. You rediscover yourself and find out that people are too blooming nosey, and are all too ready and willing to either give you advice that you don't need or trade gossip with your ex- partner. No thank you. Some do it deliberately and some do it accidentally and unintentionally, but it all has the same damaging effects. And, in reality, no matter how many 10s or even 100s of friend you think you have, you will find that most are either not worthy of your friendship or they are merely acquaintances that like to call you a friend. I have news: you only really have two or three real friends in your life. Tough. Deal with it.

The other strange thing about friends is that you really don't know who they are. You think you have the perfect trusting friend that will never ever rat or run out on you... 'There's no bloody way he or she would do that', 'I'd trust him or her with my life' ... Wrong!!! I may not represent the norm, but from my experience a true friend comes from the strangest of angles and the oddest of encounters; people that you would not have banked on as your true friends are always in the background, hovering like your very own guardian angels. I am so lucky to have so many guardian angels that I love unconditionally. In my head, I have a hypothetical statement that I would put to someone to discover whether they are indeed a true friend or just and acquaintance. Fortunately, I have never had to broach this hypothetical statement to anyone, but never say never.

A true friend can be determined by the response they would give to this statement: 'Look, I've lost my job, I'm in a real mess, I'm now homeless and I just need somewhere to stay and for someone to look after me for a while.' If, in your mind and judgement, they say 'yes' without hesitation, you know they are worth everything you have to give – they are a true friend. Throughout my life I've been in some states – you are responsible only for yourself, so I would say that they are all of my own doing – but I've always picked myself up. I can tell you that there are some wonderful people out there. These people ask no questions, they are just true souls.

Finally, with references cleared and my deposit and first month's advance rent paid up, I moved into the house in Yardley. I had kept my cool, acting like a responsible person that you would rent a house out to, but when I got behind closed doors, I went into a tailspin. Down and down I went into hell itself.

I got back to my house one day and went straight to bed, but soon woke up coughing and in a really bad way. I was itching just below the underside of each of my armpits, and when I looked in the mirror I saw some large raised zit-type lumps. I squeezed them and out came a milky white substance. I didn't know it at the time, but they were raised lymph glands. I had been coughing up – and suffocating on – copious amounts of thick green phlegm. The suffocating and coughing continued for days, and I became very weak. I still got up every day, stubbornly refusing to miss a shift at work. I would cough constantly, bringing up loads of phlegm. Fortunately, I was out in the car for most of the day, so I arrived early, came back late to sign out, and dashed off before anyone at my work could speak to me.

The raised lymph nodes itched so badly that my skin was getting sore, but slowly settled down. The coughing continued with a passion, but the volume of phlegm abated to only a small amount. This went on for about eight weeks, and then it started to clear up, soon becoming a distant memory.

I didn't go to see a doctor as I wasn't worth it – I lived only for my little dog Jess. Without her, I really couldn't give a shit if I lived or died. Every trip up the stairs I looked at that loft hole, until, eventually, I knew I had to move out of that confined space. The big flowery 70s wallpaper was suffocating my brain-cells.

It was all those years of built-up stress coming out of me, I'm sure it was, and however hard I tried to become a tree in those weeks, I couldn't. Not having that escape was a great loss to me, and I was glad to get the ability back and start working on breathing out the bad stuff.

I searched out a house that was less oppressive. Somewhere that I thought would be good for me, somewhere I could breath, grow and concentrate on my quest, and somewhere that didn't have a beckoning loft hatch at the top of the flowery carpeted avenue of stairs. I looked up at it every time I went up or down the stairs. As luck would have it, I got stuck in traffic one day on my way home from work – the M42 motorway was closed between junctions 4 and 5 due to a road traffic accident. I took the backroads and predictably I got horribly lost due to my rubbish sense of direction… Bingo. Lovely. I went down Addington Road in Hockley Heath, and there was a board up saying 'To Let' outside an end-terraced ex-municipal property. I called the letting agent – miraculously the man was in the area – I viewed it there and then and agreed to take it on at the earliest convenience. Everything went through swimmingly and I moved in.

I had a six-month tenancy at the house on Preston Road, but I really didn't care; it was so oppressive and was strangling me from the inside out. I just called the utility companies with final meter readings and told the landlord to keep the deposit – I would have drowned if I had stayed any longer. My new house was good for me. I had space, my little doggie Jess had air to breath and I was alive. I lived. Jess and I walked miles down the country lanes and across fields. My depression was so deep and dark I found it difficult to raise my head, let alone smile, but I continued to work until the contract I had came to an end. After that I took five weeks off and got myself back on track. My depression was still really bad, but with my morale lifted and my demeanour changed for the better, I was on the mend. I could now concentrate on my quest to find my lost family.

So, with new found confidence and gusto, I decided to try and trace my real family. I really had no idea of how to do it, I'd never been within twenty paces of a computer and I'd never spoken to anyone about how to go about putting my first foot on the ancestral-chasing ladder. The only tips I had had come from stuff I'd seen on the TV, mainly *Heir Hunters*. So off I went on my quest with clarity and confidence almost geysering out of me.

On the advice of a friend, I went to the library to look at and trawl the microfiche records. I saw the lady at the counter and she gave me basic instructions on how to operate the microfiche machine. It was really simple when I got the hang of it, but so laborious.

The Librarian asked me, 'In what location do you want to search in and in what time period?'

'I really don't know,' I replied to the bemused librarian, who was trying her best to help me. I should have at least brought a pen and paper with me, and had a rough idea of dates.

I showed the lady my crumpled up birth certificate and told her that I was trying to find my mother and father, whose names were listed on the certificate. I told the lady I had no idea if my mother or father were still alive. I believe at one point I had been told my father was dead, but without proof I really didn't know. All I had was a black and white school photograph and my birth certificate to work with. I had no family to tell me whether my memories were true or false, fact or fiction. Patiently the librarian accommodated me, giving me some more advice and loading the microfiche machine up with the relevant microfiche cards.

I trawled and trawled, I went back day after day, week after week, writing reference numbers, and just ended up getting more and more confused about the whole process. I was impatient. When I start doing something, I try to go in head-first and complete it. It was frightening but impressive, the amount of work I did in such a small window of time. Time and again, I asked for new microfiche cards, but I wasn't really getting anywhere. I did find a Horace Lawton who had died in Oswestry in 1970 – who later turned out to be my father – but I dismissed the record because of the location and his young age of 44 years. I didn't remember when I went into care, so I assumed I must have been about three or four years old at the time and estimated my father's age to be around 30 when he died, if he had died at all. I trawled for 'Angela Mary Lawton' and found no one that stood out as my mother.

Were they both still alive? Were they looking for me too? What lies have they been told? Did I have brothers and sisters? So many unanswered questions kept popping into my head – they were eating me from the inside out.

I was stuck in a continuous loop. I had no idea how to progress from where I was. The Librarian advised that I take down the reference numbers and go to Town Hall to look at records and order birth, marriage and death certificates. But it was all way too complicated for me. What, was I supposed to order thousands of certificates? The patient lady then asked if I had tried the internet and told me that there were new websites that would undoubtable help me. She wrote down the names of the websites for me, and I thanked her for her time and patience. I was done with the library, although it had been of some help to me, forming the foundation of my search.

With the advice I received from the librarian, I went out and bought a laptop so that I could enlist on one of the ancestry websites that she had written down for me. But with such limited information, I found that I was saving and printing off loads of stuff whilst not getting anywhere at all. I really needed cast-iron dates and names to progress further. I persisted and kept slowly typing in dates and names, prodding away robotically with my one-finger typing technique. Eventually it all came to a head. Although the website was more user-friendly than the microfiche machine, it was not helping me at all. If only I could get one lead… If only I knew proper dates and names… I sorted out my printed pages into chronological order, and then looked for physical help.

I attempted to meet someone in person who traced people's families for a living. I searched on the computer by typing in 'family tree' and 'ancestor tracing', even finding that to be traumatic. I didn't really know what was what, and I found myself just writing down lots of phone numbers, addresses and titles. My brain cells were so frazzled by this stage that I nearly gave up the ghost. Utterly dismayed and disillusioned, I left it all for a week or two to ponder on how to go forward. I didn't want to tell anyone or discuss my search with anyone I knew, as I had kept my secret past life hidden from all but a few very close friends. The last thing I wanted to do was expose myself to those closest to me. Eventually I called a couple of the phone numbers I had written down weeks earlier. Most went to dead tones and some went straight to voicemail, which, by the way, I wasn't at all prepared for. I was close to giving up again. I had work to do, money to earn and all of the researching was taking a big hit not only on my mental health but on my finances. It was also affecting my work and it was showing. My search was all-consuming and I needed to get a grip on reality and perhaps give up altogether.

My list of ancestry-searching phone numbers was low, and I knew I had to give it one very last try. My morale was low, and I really didn't hold out much hope in progressing any further in my search for my family. I blamed myself big-time. *What do you expect after leaving it for nearly fifty years, Keith?* I went on to myself, tumbling into depression and self-deprecation. I was really just generally giving myself a hard time. I decided that I would rehearse a reply if I was met by a voicemail message when I made another enquiry. This had been my main stumbling block. 'I'm a construction worker, not a blooming secretary,' I told myself. So I rehearsed some spiel to spout out if met by a pre-recorded voicemail message.

Finally, I got the courage up to go off in my break time and try calling the last few telephone numbers I had left. I found a quiet place in the local park, sat down, opened my wallet and produced the crumpled up piece of paper that I had written the numbers on. There were only three left at the bottom of the page that weren't crossed out. Dialling the first on my mobile, I got another pissing voicemail. I spouted out my pre-rehearsed reply and pressed the end of call button. Then I got up off my bench, I was so fed up, and I threw the piece of paper containing the numbers into the rubbish bin. Being totally dismayed with the whole process, I gave up. 'At least I have tried,' I told myself.

About three days later, two missed call showed up on my mobile phone. I worked outside in all weathers, usually covered from head to toe in mud, and had to wear gloves on account of the rough work, so my mobile phone was tucked inside a plastic bag inside my coat to protect it from the weather, the dust and knocks. My head was splitting – I was so mad I had missed those calls, but at least I knew I had received calls. I really didn't know where they were from though, because I hadn't saved any of the phone numbers, and my bit of paper was long gone. I didn't wait until lunchtime to make my return call, as I had to do it straight away. So I asked my workmate Tommy O'Sullivan to cover for me while I slipped off-site to make a call. To my delight and amazement, Jeannette answered straight away; she told me that she had picked up my voicemail and was returning my call. She had been away for a week, and told me she was sorry. I was overjoyed to hear back from someone, and I could feel that she was the right person for me. Eager to see Jeannette as soon as I could, I asked if she could text message me her address, a time that was convenient for her, what I needed to take with me and what the whole thing would cost.

The day came for me to meet Jeannette, and off I went along with my computer print outs and my crumpled-up, dog-eared birth certificate. Predictably, upon meeting this person and sitting down at her table, I found it impossible to do anything but ramble incoherently and tearfully. Eventually, after tea, sympathy and being departed of £600, I was assured that I would hear from the researcher within three weeks. Jeannette assured me that she would have no problem finding my true family – if they lived or even if they had passed away – as long as they were in the country. She explained that on my birth certificate was a unique reference number that would ensure her research was valid.

With the weeks passing and my mind racing, I knew I had to concentrate on my work to try and take my mind off things. I had failed miserably with my futile searches for my birth family, and I knew from past experience that if you fail you have to admit it, put it behind you, learn from it and move on. Working in the construction industry has one common trait: when things are finished being built, you usually get laid off, and so I was well used to getting laid off and looking for new work. This is also like a failure in a way. Basically, you put it behind you and move forward having learned something new. My new contract did indeed take my mind off things. I was and still am a total sceptic, and I didn't expect to get any news from Jeannette Carter the ancestry researcher I'd given £600 to. If anything, I was half-expecting a call asking for more money as the search was proving more difficult than she had first envisaged. What I didn't know before Jeannette told me was about the unique reference number that was on my birth certificate that categorically linked my birth parents to me. I held this information as hope that I would hear from Jeannette soon. The waiting was painful.

I was very surprised when, finally, I got a call from Jeannette. The news came and it tore me apart, but there was also hope in what she told me. My father had died in Oswestry in 1970 at the age of 44 years. Receiving this news was like getting hit by a truck, even though it was something I was prepared for. Jeannette, sensing my pain, asked me if I was okay. She asked if I wanted her to go on, or if I'd rather she just sent it all to me in the mail. I wanted her to go on, I wanted to know more. I wanted to know where my mother lived and if I had any brothers and sisters.

Jeannette then went on to tell me that my mother had died of cancer in a care home in Clacton-on-Sea, Essex back in 2007 at the age of 71 years. The pain hit me like a bolt of lightning. I felt weak, sick, hungry, tired, ill, shocked and so much hurt I cannot describe… But there was more to come, and my torment wasn't over. Jeannette hadn't quite finished, and went on to inform me that my older brother Brian had died in Torquay back in 2004 at the young age of 44 years. It bloody hurt so badly, but I wanted to know about other siblings…

Where's my sister? I know I have a sister, I can feel it… Where does she live? How old is she? Is she married?

Jeannette said, 'I didn't find a sister, Keith. You don't appear to have a sister. But you do have another brother called Stephen, and I cannot find records for his death, so I assume that he's still alive.' I cannot remember how many times I said thank you to Jeannette, and I still to this day thank her from right down deep in my soul. I am also convinced that I have a sister, despite being told by others that I don't. I can feel it. I know I have a sister, but where is she? I will find her eventually. This is something else that will continue to torture me, and I will never give up on her – unless she finds me first.

I then went back online and gained the death certificates of my parents and my brother. I ordered birth and death certificates like they were going out of fashion, but I needed the tangible proof. I was thirsty for the truth after being lied to for all of my life, both by people who did it deliberately, and others, do-gooders, who thought that the truth would hurt me, and tried to protect me from it. Let me tell you one thing: the lies and the not knowing hurt a damn sight more.

So there I had it in front of me in black and white: my father had died in 1970. He had been a painter, and he had fallen from a ladder and broken his back, leading to his death from a heart attack. A man way too young to be taken away from his family. And to think he died in a bid to get money to support his young family of three boys, all under 11 years old, and wife of 33. The news of this put to bed one of the many confusing, frightening things in my life. I then realised that my nightmares, my constant visualisations featuring a man strapped to a wheeled hospital bed, screaming, looking right into my eyes, were indeed true all along. After seeing my father's death certificate, I can recall this event with true clarity. My mother was there but my two brothers were not – I now remember it so clearly, it's like it happened yesterday. You see, my two brothers would have been at school, and I was with my mother because I was too young for school. It's not the best single memory for a child to have of his father branded into his mind, but it has now faded away from my psyche and that is something I am grateful for, I can assure you.

I got the details of my mother's place of death from her death certificate, which was among the many I ordered, and I wrote to the care home where she had passed away. A woman there kindly sent me a long letter explaining what a wonderful lady my mother was and that they all miss her terribly. Enclosed were three photographs which I treasure beyond all things. A copy of this letter by Joan Owens is transcribed below, word for word:

Regent House
Clacton-on-Sea
12th June 2012

Dear Keith,

I was very saddened to receive your letter about yourself and Angela. Angela was a very special lady to us. She was kind, and very quiet and had a good sense of humour.

As you are probably aware, she was a troubled lady – as in her mental health. She was very private and we were unaware of her history or background until after her death.

Angela missed you boys, that's all we did know, she mentioned your names as Stephen, Keith and Brian – but we did not really know if you existed, apart from Stephen who placed her here in social services.

Stephen brought Angela down here from the north. He had lived in Colchester with her, and he was married at some point and had a son.

Angela had been unwell with breast cancer, she had become unwell and he had found it difficult to cope, that is our understanding.

Stephen sometimes visited at odd times, and sometimes we did not know he was here. Angela was very fond of her grandson and longed to see him.

Stephen's visits grew further apart and we learned of his divorce after which he was not around much.

For a few years prior to your mum's death, he had been in the States – we only found this out later.

Angela was very happy with us and seemed settled. She was a very private and quiet person. She became unwell with her tummy extending – but would not go to the hospital or have any tests or treatment. All she would say is, 'There is no point, it's more of the same.' The GP tried to convince her but she was having none of it. She was a force to be reckoned with and once her mind was made up, no one could change it.

I started to try and find Stephen when Angela became unwell, and I was unsuccessful. Over a 100 Stephen

Lawton letters later, I had no choice but to leave it. We had informed the police of this urgency but to no avail (later finding out that Stephen was out of the country).

We moved Angela to the ground floor and a member of staff was with her at all times. She was on appropriate medication and was in no pain. She passed away at 10:20am on the 23rd of September 2007, age 71 years. Two staff were with her and she departed peacefully.

We knew Angela wished to be buried and she is laid to rest in Burrs Cemetery, Burrs Road, Great Clacton. Mr R. Gwinnell and Sons Funeral Directors conducted the funeral for us and a reading was written by my night staff, who was very close to her and read at her graveside. The death was registered by me, and I can apologise here and now because I was unaware she lived in the north. That is why Colchester is on the document as her birth place.

After a couple of years, a card arrived for Angela with an address. I found a phone number and phoned the person on the card, and it was Angela's sister-in-law. I'm sure they lived in Birmingham or that area. Angela has brothers and family around the place she lived when married. I cannot remember the lady's name – and have nothing to look up.

She informed me that Angela had been happily married, but her husband had died. I think he fell off a roof.

Angela had suffered from depression before, and losing her husband made her unwell. She lost you boys as she was not coping, and was taken into hospital.

Last year Angela's grandson came to see her at the weekend, as he was about 16. He was told by staff that she had passed away and we were trying to contact Stephen.

Stephen came to see me last year, explaining his divorce and his travels. I gave him the folder with his aunts' and uncles' details and the death certificate, the reading and all of the details of trying to find him that I had gathered. So I have nothing to offer you but some pictures I have found in our photo albums. We do not have many as Angela was shy and did not like being in them. The last one being with her key worker Sue, who she got on well with.

Stephen's son still lives in Colchester with his mother. I cannot tell you where Stephen is now, he has always been allusive.

I am sorry I haven't got more to give you, but ring if you want to chat.

All I can say is Angela was a grand lady. She was gentle and kind and never stopped missing you boys.

Kind Regards,
Joan Owens

I will be forever grateful to Joan Owens for writing this letter, and one day I hope to find the strength within me to go down and thank her for it in person. One day I also hope to thank Sue for composing a reading, and for reading it over my mother's grave.

And above all, one day I really hope I can muster up enough composure from deep within my soul to visit my mother's grave, and to arrange to get a headstone placed there. It's definitely no less than anyone deserves, least of all my mum.

I can tell you for sure, whether I finish this book or not, I do believe that the people at Regent House, that cared for my mother at the place she was happiest, should be the first to receive a copy of this book. They should hear the truth of what happened to Angela Mary Lawton, their Angela, written by one of her boys, before the story gets lost.

I even ordered my own birth certificate despite the fact that I already had a crumpled copy, for I needed to verify that it was a true document. The satanic Mrs Davenport only did one decent thing for me: when I left the children's home, she gave me a little folder with an old school photograph and my birth certificate. Incredibly, it took this long for me to discover my own birth date. Both of these I kept from my foster parents for all of those years, an attitude that is remnant of being brought up in council care. Don't tell anyone your secrets, because they will no longer be secrets, and don't tell anyone you have something hidden, because the next time you look it will no longer be there. Foolishly, I made this mistake with my mother's letter and my father's photograph. But I didn't recognise how important they were at that time, and so I do forgive myself for that one error.

The researcher sent me a host of information through the post – it was the best £600 I'd ever spent. She gave me a list of Stephen Lawton's voting records, and off I went, writing and posting ten generic letters a day, containing a brief description and my mobile phone number. I waited a week before sending out another batch. This went on for weeks, and I must have sent a hundred letters when I got a distraught phone call from someone saying that the person I was looking for was her dad. Her father had never mentioned that he had a brother and he'd died two years earlier. Thankfully the age of her Stephen didn't match up with mine.

Eventually I did receive a phone call from my brother and I went to see him in Nottingham that weekend. His son Dominick was with him at the time, and he rarely visited, so that was a stroke of luck. I received the call whilst I was at work, and I knew it was him straight away, but it was someone I didn't know so I was very careful. I said I was at work and that I'd call later, which I did. I really needed time to compose myself and to keep my mind still. I became a tree, I became a tree about five times in fact, and then I felt ready to ring Stephen back.

What do you say to a brother who you don't know? What do you ask a brother who was brought up by different people? What do you say to a brother when you don't know what he looks like? Where do you start?

Stephen knew our mother Angela had died, but it was a shock to him that our brother Brian had passed away at the young age of 44. Brian had probably died of a broken heart, being the eldest, and seeing and knowing what had happened to our dad, unlike me. He also witnessed the injustices that had been done to our poor mother in Blackpool. She paid the price of a life sentence, being incarcerated and having her family – her air – taken away from her, while those animals went away free. Hopefully the men that hurt her have it in them to repent, and karma has made them suffer as my poor mother – and the rest of my family – did. I'm sure all of this killed my older brother at such a young age.

The men that hurt my mother need to stand before their god and confess all in a court of law. Then they should be made accountable for their actions and suffer the consequences of them. They should be made to sit in the chute that sends them down below to the horned red man with the trident, to be poked and prodded for an eternity whilst feeling the severe heat of the hellfire on their sorry bodies. Like all monsters, they continue to haunt their victims and the families of their victims, and like all monsters, they see themselves as normal, they see power in not confessing and will never relinquish that power. They cannot admit that their actions were wrong

– not even to themselves. So let the fire consume them, it's the only way. Don't spend one penny of hard working people's tax money to lock them up, allowing them to carry on breathing the same air as decent people. They'll just pollute it.

After drinking myself into a stupor for many years to block out the pain, it brings me strength to know that I was never a natural drinker nor smoker, and it has been a long time since I have used either as a refuge. I can also say that alcohol doesn't block out the pain at all in any way. It is a depressant and only compounds pain and misery, and gives the man that lurks below a chance to invade your mind and soul. It is in no way a right or moral path in which to follow, and it is important to be responsible enough to face your own problems head on and to deal with them. However steep the mountain seems, you can climb it.

Grave Relatives

With the new information giving me cast-iron dates, I made phone calls in an attempt to find my father's grave. My brother Stephen wasn't much help in this search, so I relied on the facts that I had on my father's death certificate. Finally, after multiple telephone calls and more waiting, I got a place and a grave number. I only found my dad's grave two years ago. I can tell you that it is pure torture not knowing whether your dad is alive or dead, and then, after finding out he is dead, not knowing where he was laid to rest. I can also say that it brings me great peace to talk to him in hours of difficulty. I spent hours cleaning the grave that had been neglected for over forty-five years, and you wouldn't believe the amount of bleach and the number of toothbrushes I got through. A very strange thing happened to me before I found my dad's grave. It really knocked me down and changed my way of thinking. In fact, it really changed my way of life.

Off I went to Bilston Cemetery. It was a lovely, bright sunny day, and I had longed to find my father's place of rest so that I could sit, cry, pray and most of all chat away to him. I parked my car, walked up and down between the graves, and looked at the names on the headstones. I saw the keeper, but I really wanted to find it myself. I felt a presence, and I knew his grave was there somewhere. I had been trawling cemeteries for years, and was well versed in methodically walking up and down the rows of headstone, reading names and peeling back vegetation. Although I had been there before, that day was different. Now that the lady had told me he was buried there, there was something else… Something very strong was happening deep inside of me.

Then, unbeknownst to me, I began to near my dad's grave, and the heavens opened – I mean it really rained hard. I darted off to my car, and all of the time I felt my phone vibrating. As I was in the car, dripping wet, I reached into my trouser pocket for my phone. Now I know this might have happened because my phone had gotten wet, but I had 132 text messages showing in my inbox, and they were all from the same person, Dave Gooding. They were all blank. Dave is no relation but I did work with him. I spoke to Dave on the following Monday at work, and I told him that he'd been sending me blank text messages over the weekend. He said that he had left his work phone at home all weekend – as it was his work phone – while he went away with his wife and kids, because he didn't want to be disturbed. But really, I do not see how you could accidently send that many texts anyway, so I think it was my dad's way of saying, 'Come back, son, I'm here, you've found me.'

I waited for the rain to abate, it went away as quickly as it came, and then I went straight to the keeper, who was extremely helpful. The keeper got out some laminated A1 scape drawings of the plots, with individual graves and grave numbers. We went to the grave, and it was in such a state we couldn't see the writing. I would have walked passed it a hundred times and not have seen it. The keeper had worked there for many years, and was adept at finding the slightest obscure inscriptions, and there it was on the side of the grave: 'Also his brother, Horace Lawton, died June 6th, 1970, aged 44 years.'

The keeper left me in peace, confronted with my father's family grave and with my head bowed. It rained, again, and I took some pictures with my sodden mobile phone and then left. I returned to the grave the following weekend, along with my brother Stephen and some flowers. I left Stephen alone at Dad's grave to chat to him as I had done, then we both left and went to the pub to have a drink for our dad, something we had been denied before. We also grieved. Stephen, being about ten years old when Dad died, told me what he remembered of him, my mum and my brother Brian.

I came back to my dad's grave the following weekend and have done every weekend after that, and I cleaned the grave to its' former state. I laid flowers, I laid a plaque for my mother and brother, and I left my contact details sealed in a plastic bag. No one ever called.

I then unexpectedly received a message on Facebook from a woman who turned out to be my mother's sister. She asked, 'Is this Keith Lawton, Angela's son?' So I replied and wrote back. The care home must have written to her, as my mother was apparently a prolific letter writer. This of course led to friend requests from some members of my real family that knew about me, but I didn't know about them. Then one day I received a friend request from a woman called Anne. She also asked me if I was Angela's son, to which I replied yes. It turned out that Anne was no relation of mine, but she had been my mother's friend when she was younger and married. Anne asked if I would like to meet her at the Hollybush garden centre in Willenhall, Wolverhampton. I was of course hungry for any information I could find out about my mother.

I met Anne at the garden centre and she told me some things she thought I should know, things that really helped me, things that I am forever grateful to her for telling me. Then suddenly Anne dropped a bombshell: she had some people for me to meet. My legs like jelly, we sat at a table, talked for a while, and then two elderly people came in and sat with us. Anne said, 'This is Chris, your mum's brother and Cathy, his wife.' We exchanged some history, I gained some more photographs, which I think you can never have too many of, and me and Anne left.

I thanked Anne and I said I wanted to get some stuff for my garden. She walked around the shop with me, and I gained more information and insight into why and how I ended up in a council care home.

Anne told me what had happened to my mother, and what those animals did to her in Blackpool during her time of grieving. She also told me what she knew of what happened after that, and how Mum was taken into an asylum straight from the train. Anne explained that my mother was a prolific letter writer, and she wrote to all of her sisters and brothers, all of the time, which of course begs the question as to why, even in her later dying years, no one went to see her or tried to look after her.

Anne gave me insight into my mother's family, and how she was stigmatised and kept out of the way because of her illness. Heaven forbid they would have to be associated with her. This was stuff she knew, stuff that was locked into the family, into the bigoted mind-set of 1950s to 1970s people. The people who allowed me and my brothers to be incarcerated and exposed to evil.

The realisation hit me afterwards that, although they had found me after all those years, they still weren't interested in me much like they weren't interested in my mum. I was a bad smell that could possibly drag up the past and expose those unfeeling hypocrites for what they were… But I wasn't about to do that. I'd achieved what I had set out to do, and now it was their turn to offer the olive branch – but of course it never came.

This was stuff that set me free from years of torment, and it still took me a long time to write it down. It is still extremely raw and it still punishes me daily. Eventually I had to cut those people out of my loop, and I thank Anne wholeheartedly for bringing her suspicions to my attention, and clarifying and rejuvenating some distant memories that eventually came flooding back with great clarity, releasing my soul. I have still got a long bumpy road to travel, but light is there and eventually I will make it.

Back to Normal

With the professional help of Jeanette and her team of researchers, I finally, after all of those years of not knowing, knew the true path my life had taken in those early years. Getting all of it into perspective gave me the building blocks to help me start moving forward... 'You gotta get up to get down.' It also became apparent to me during my quest that it is something you cannot do alone, and I would advise the reader to get professional advice from someone who helps people find their families for a living.

I was extremely lucky in meeting Jeannette, and if you don't feel you have the right person for you, then move on, as with anything in life. The Good Lord gave us arms, legs and a mind, so take your gut feeling and just walk away. I really wish someone had given me that advice long ago, because it would have saved me an awful lot of heartache and grief. I was all too mistrusting of people, but there are a lot of people out there that will give you some really good advice. You may not choose to hear it when you're first told it, but it sometimes triggers stuff in you that helps you choose the right path. I have since received my file from social services, and made all of the changes I needed to. I was not very far from the truth, but I do wish I knew I could apply for it before I first started writing, as it would have saved me an awful lot of time. But hey – it has all been very worthwhile to me.

I have worked in civil engineering ever since and I see it as my industry. One thing about the people that work in the industry is that they are totally accepting of who you are, and they employ everyone from illegals to ex-offenders without any questions and without any judgement. You are valued based on your own merit and your own efforts. There are no gender, race or nationality stigmas in the civil engineering, and that is what makes it a good, eclectic, vibrant industry.

Nobody knows everything, and we have all got a lot to learn from each other as inhabitants of this planet. There is still aloof hypocrisy in the civil engineering industry, as there is in all industries – which comes from the remnants of the class system. This attitude comes mainly from project managers, quantity surveyors and health and safety professionals – none of which I would even trust with a Lego set. Nevertheless, their refusal to learn from people that know the industry inside out – the people on the ground that do the job – is their own misfortune. It also seems that those same types of people are oblivious to the basic fact that none of it matters in relation to the bigger picture. We are all naked in the bathroom and God gave each of us a hole to crap through, so I have news: we are all the same and we all breathe, eat and shit. It's ironic that most of those who think that they are above everyone else have come from working class backgrounds like me. People who are well-bred, so to speak, have a quality about them, and they are not pretentious in the main. So there's the irony.

All people deserve a decent day's pay for a decent day's work, and in the construction industry, that is what you get. You are only judged on your ability to turn out good work, or your ability to turn out rubbish work and to turn out a lot of it. There are places for everyone, but no places for bullying, racism and machos. People who walk around site as if they have got a cardboard box under each arm, and one between their legs, are just inexperienced people and don't realise how daft they look. They are a danger to themselves and everyone else, but it always comes out of them in time. It really would be a rubbish world if every sweet contained in a box of Quality Street were the same.

The construction industry houses them all, from nut-job to odd-job, from the incapable to the extremely capable. Every type of person at every end of the scale – you look and they are there. I have seen men come on-site with nothing and they leave quite well off. I've also seen people who were formerly well off, and were contractors themselves, come to the site with nothing, to start over again. No one questions them, takes the mickey out of them or otherwise – they are just one of the lads again. Basically, you gotta get up to get down.

The construction industry became my family, and the Irish community of Birmingham became my extended family. On more than one occasion some old Irish man has told me that he wished his son was just like me, that I should be very proud of myself for being so well turned out, or that, if he had a son, he would want him to be just like me. It is difficult to tell you how I feel on these occasions – such words warm my heart and give me comfort. I used to keep it all inside my head until I wrote this book, and I am glad I kept it all in. Not only because I relive it all as I write, but because I am also able to share my thoughts with the reader, who may just go on to tell their own story one day. They might help to sway the tide of people's opinions, break down the stereotypical views of people with entrenched mind-sets and change the world for the better.

The construction industry houses some very clever individuals indeed, and I will never leave it. I still work in the industry today, although I wield a pen and not a hammer.

Throughout the years, I have repeatedly observed the same human behavioural changes in the industry and I am very proud of that fact. I still live in Birmingham, as I love the West Midlands, and I love the people's humour and their down-to-earthiness. I love the fact that the West Midlands is so spread out and diverse, and that there are a myriad of different towns and different high streets, all with different architecture and all with different people, bars, cafés, shops, cultures and foods. There are areas that are the pinnacle of development, and other parts where things haven't changed for years on end. There are vibrant backstreets that house ancient artisan businesses that thrive, but seem like they have been forgotten by time. It is these things that make it for me.

From being a general labourer, to becoming a ganger-man, to foreman, then to general foreman, I managed to work my way up in the industry. I have worked on roads, bridges, high-rise blocks, and been deep down underground in sewers, basements and tunnels. I continue to learn, read and take various courses, as I think learning and the ability to learn is a wonderful gift. My work has taken me to different parts of the country and even abroad, and has been filled with varied projects. Eventually I found a path that suited me, my morals, my ethics and just who I am generally. I now lean towards quality and health and safety within the construction industry. For the last two years, I have worked in Manchester on a major highways scheme in quality assurance. I have a year left in the position, and then it's back to working in my beloved West Midlands. I must add that since I've worked in Manchester, I've discovered that people travel to Wolverhampton by train, just to stop off and listen to the station announcer's accent before travelling back home after having had a side-splitting day... Joking, of course.

I have deleted all of my so-called blood relatives' details. After being in contact with them, writing emails,

I found that all our conversations were one way. I was in contact with members of my family for nearly two years. Some aunties, uncles and cousins never even wrote to me, and during the whole time I was never invited to any family occasion – not a birthday, christening or anniversary. I was so looking forward to getting just one invite and meeting members of my real family. It consumed me. It was like another form of control, so I just took the initiative, cut ties with them and got on with my own life. I wasn't letting them hold me to ransom with the one-way conversations, just as they had done to my poor mother for years by not responding to her letters. I am not a bitter person, but quite frankly it is their loss. My morals are better than theirs, and yes, I win again.

It has been a long time since I worked for Brian Binton in Torquay, or indeed for Andy Finley in Birmingham, but I learned a lot about my trade, about people and life in those years I spent with them. And I learned so many different things from peoples' antics and humour. True, honest people, many of whom have long since passed on to another world. May they rest in peace.

Still, the one person that I remember the most, as I thought it was so comical at the time, was Chris Finnegan and his bottle of cider that he had buried in the sand on a hot summer's day to try and keep it cool. As he laid back and drank his cider without a care in the world, he took the power away from his tormentor. And as he walked off-site towards the pub, sticking his middle finger up to Andy Finley, he released the burden of his torment and turned it into a humorous memory. That was the day Chris Finnegan won.

There is a lesson in Chris Finnegan's actions for everyone: just walk away. You are always far better than your tormentor, and they are the weak-minded ones in trying to gain attention through other people's misery.

Postscript

One thing I have learned from my life is that no matter how you look after your child, nurturing them and protecting them from the things that you do not want them to be exposed to, there is always someone lurking, watching and waiting for that chance to lead the fruit of your labours into bad ways. Whether its people of the same age, abusers, skilled manipulators or people online, they are there, waiting for their opportunity. It doesn't matter how you try to protect them or what your social standing, class or awareness is, they will still watch and wait for that chink of light in the door, so that they can slowly drive a wedge in and gain access. Unfortunately, no matter how remote you think you are from it, it still happens. It is a cruel world we live in. There is one other thing I would like to add, and that is that kids of today seem to be almost protected too much. They don't go out and walk for miles, or go out on their bikes for hours on end, or even go out to play as much nowadays. But the thing I'm trying to get at, something I have learned throughout my life, mainly from my time in the construction industry, is that you have to be exposed to a certain level of risk to be able to appreciate future risk.

The main lesson I have learned from my own experiences in life is that it does not matter whether a child is brought up in a privileged environment or on a rough council estate... Creeds, abilities and nationalities, none of them makes a person better or worse than anyone else, and it doesn't stop them from being targeted any more or any less than anyone else is. Posh kids go to jail too. The one thing that does protect them is their own DNA, their internal moral standing and nothing much else. The one thing that drives kids away is lack of or too much attention, people stereotyping them and people's expectations of them.

Over the years, I have read a few books similar to this one and my debut book *No Photographs*, as I have had an affinity with the subject due to my upbringing in council care homes. Most books I read were based in Ireland – relating to the Sisters of Mercy and the Christian Brothers – but some were based in the UK and other countries. These accounts all have similar connotations, and it begs the question as to why, with so many people giving testimonies about past injustices, that they are never fully recognised and brought out in the open. Such occurrences are also brought to our attention on what almost seems like a daily basis through all sorts of media. I feel that if you wanted to question two people to ascertain holes in their stories, then you would separate them, and ask them both the same questions. And by doing this – to a certain extent – you should be able to highlight whether one or both were not telling the truth.

In the case of the accounts and testimonies given through the many books written by people who have been in one institution or another, there is a clear consistency and correlation to be seen. If so many people's accounts are unrelated, then it proves categorically that the events did indeed take place. There is stigma attached to the subjects that these books focus on, and so aloof, bigoted attitudes obstinately refuse to believe or accept the accounts given. Who is wrong?

It is difficult to put these things to paper. You open your heart and tell these stories in a bid to both draw attention to them, and to help other people who have been in similar situations, but in doing this you also leave yourself vulnerable. You tell people what has happened to you and some cannot accept it, some no longer want to be associated with you, even though they might not say it out loud. And although it is to some extent cathartic to write these stories down, it dredges up feelings that you have spent all of your life trying to suppress and forget. I applaud anyone who has the sheer guts and determination to enable themselves to write a book and bring these subjects to the attention of a wider audience, raising awareness and preventing certain people from committing these crimes against humanity.

There's only one piece of advice I'd give: no matter how much money or influence you have, you can never buy back one second of yesterday. So never dwell on the past or look to the future, because neither will have any real influence on your life. This moment is all you can live for. Learn to move on from yesterday, live and love for today, and tomorrow is only tomorrow when and if tomorrow comes.

Acknowledgements

Firstly, I would like to thank Jeannette Carter for doing such thorough professional work during my initial search for my family. Without Jeannette's help, I would not have gotten anywhere close to even writing this book.

Secondly, I would like to thank Joan Owens and the wonderful staff at Regency House in Clacton-on-Sea. They gave my mother peace, love, affection and the highest pinnacle of care I could have ever wished for. I also thank Joan for her heartfelt letter, which is something I will always keep close to me and gain great comfort from. She also arranged my mother's burial and conducted readings over her grave, which means so much to me that I cannot put it into words.

Thirdly, I would like to thank Wolverhampton County Council for keeping records and for digging out the file of my time in council care. The information held within was invaluable to me not only because it helped me piece together this book, but because it helped my mental health and gave me facts, dates and clarity.

Of course I'd like to thank the reader in advance of their feedback, and any arguments or debates that they raise from the confines of this book. I'd also like to applaud anyone that this book has helped, either in changing their life or in convincing them to tell their own story. The whole point of this book is to raise awareness and help to change people's perspectives on things. It is important not to blame one's self for the actions of others, and ironically, not to blame others for their actions. Forgive, forget, move on, do not let them win and take comfort in the fact that nothing that happened was your fault.

I urge the reader to share this story, as weight in numbers will help to change things for the better. People need to lose the stigma that protects perpetrators. Change only comes from weight of numbers, and so the more people that read, the greater the chance of change.

Humbly Yours,
Keith Lawton (KeithLawton@Ymail.com)

File Notes

[Here are some extracts from my social services file. I am unable to share any more, as it is too shocking even for me to read.]

17/03/1969: (I was four years old at this time and had been monitored since I was born.)

Taken off family case work load as all three children now in care. Rang Matron, the Hollies, to arrange for clothing orders immediately. Rang Matron, the Hollies, and told her about Keith. Rang Education and Welfare.

Mr Lawton came to office and denied having given permission for children to come into care. He reeked of drink and his fingers were almost stained black with nicotine. Denied having left the children alone, and said he was only in the pub across the road.

18/03/1969: MSS Rang. As from Thursday Mr Lawton will get £9 per week. 10s is being sent to Angela.

24/03/1969: Some bedding bought and delivered to house. Mr Lawton looked quite ill and is having treatment from a doctor for his nerves. Said he hasn't visited his wife or children, and sent family allowance book back to children's department. Wants loan for MEB (Midlands Electricity Board). Gave him cash for this.

22/04/1969: Mr Lawton said he doesn't want the children back yet, as he wants to get the house straight.

He has finally got some curtains up in the house. Discussed what else he needs. Said he needs a cooker and some saucepans. Mrs X Visited last week and they talked about his wife's illness. He has taken her to the Hollies to see their children.

28/04/1969: Bedding and other things delivered to Mr Lawton. He showed me his efforts at redecorating.

30/04/1969: Mr Lawton to office. Smelled of drink. Told me that he doesn't want to drink, but his friends keep buying him pints.

19/05/1969: Mr Lawton bought new lino to cover the bare boards in the house. £5.10s. I suspect he has made a bit of money on the side. Rang the Hollies to bring the children home,

30/05/1969: Draft for £2 received. Bought food for the children with the £2.

08/06/1970: Visited Angela who looked very withdrawn. We obtained further prescription for her tablets. Went to see Keith. Angela said nothing. Keith said very little. Poor child.

18/11/1970: I visited Braybrook House this evening, conscious of the after-effect of the riot in the school this morning. I don't think he is very happy there. There are so many underlying tensions in there. I am sure that Braybrook isn't doing him any good whatsoever. He went into the boys' playroom to play cards, which he did for the rest of the evening. He was rather subdued and I think he had worn himself out in the riot earlier that day.

Again! I don't think Braybrook is doing these children any good whatsoever, in fact I think it is making them regress even further.

24/01/1971: Braybrook looked absolutely awful, there were hardly enough chairs to go around the reception hall. There was a dirty cup on the window sill, and there was no heating at all, and we were really shivering with the January cold. It was VERY VERY uninviting. I felt like I had to explain to Mrs X that this is not like the other children's homes.

02/02/1976: I advertised and re-advertised for over a year, and had no luck until Mrs Burton picked up the Lichfield Mercury Newspaper quite by accident and saw my newspaper advertisement, advertising Keith.

Keith is having a birthday party on the 4th – something which he has never had before – he is now 11 years old.

Copyhouse Press

London

Lightning Source UK Ltd.
Milton Keynes UK
UKOW02f1931061016

284668UK00001B/1/P